June, 1967
Honolulu, Hawaii

URBAN LANGUAGE SERIES

ROGER W. SHUY, GENERAL EDITOR

A SOCIOLINGUISTIC DESCRIPTION OF

DETROIT NEGRO SPEECH

WALTER A. WOLFRAM

CENTER FOR APPLIED LINGUISTICS : 1969

Library of Congress Catalog Card Number: 71-84378
Printed in the United States of America

Designed by Frank A. Rice

INTRODUCTION TO THE SERIES

The Urban Language Series is intended to make available the results of recent sociolinguistic research concerned with the position and role of language in a large metropolitan area. The series includes descriptions of certain aspects of urban language, particularly English, as well as theoretical considerations relevant to such descriptions. The series also includes studies dealing with fieldwork techniques, matters of pedagogy and relationships of urban language study to other disciplines. Where appropriate and feasible, accompanying tape recordings will be made available. Specifically excluded from consideration are aspects of English as a second language or second language learning in general.

It is hoped that the Urban Language Series will prove useful to several different kinds of readers. For the linguist, the series will provide data for the study of language performance and for the development of linguistic theory. Historically, linguists have formulated theory from individual rather than group performance. They have had to generalize about what constitutes "standard" or "non-standard" from intuitive judgments or from very limited data. This series is designed to make available large portions of language data as well as analyses in order to broaden the knowledge from which linguistic generalizations may come.

For the sociologist the series will provide access to the nature of social stratification by means of language. It

is the contention of some scholars that a person's use of
language is one of the most important cues to his social
status, age, race or sex.

For the educator, the series will offer among other
things a description of the very things which are most
crucial to the classroom—the linguistic correlates which
separate the accepted from the unaccepted.

Although the value of focussed attention on the special
problems of urban language has been recognized for some time,
relatively few substantial studies have been published. To
a certain degree, this series represents a pioneering venture
on the part of the Center for Applied Linguistics.

Roger W. Shuy
Director, Sociolinguistics Program
Center for Applied Linguistics

A SOCIOLINGUISTIC DESCRIPTION OF DETROIT NEGRO SPEECH

PREFACE

During the past several years we have witnessed an increasing interest in the speech of lower socio-economic class Negroes. Although the focus on that variety of English which shows the most structural and functional contrast with standard English is certainly understandable, it has now become apparent that there is a need to study the speech of a wider representation of the black population. If we are to understand the significance of speech as an indicator of status in the black community and to understand its role in social mobility, the study of the speech of Negroes must include different social groups of Negroes. The present volume is an attempt to broaden the sociolinguistic parameter of the speech of Negroes by correlating speech differences with social differences.

In this description Detroit is chosen as a case study of a large Northern urban area which has shown a dramatic increase in its Negro population within the last half century. Although the details of sociolinguistic analysis may differ from city to city, it is expected that the general outline of this description will be applicable to a number of other Northern metropolitan areas. The study reported here was begun under a contract with the Cooperative Research Branch of the U.S. Office of Education in 1966-1967 and completed under a Carnegie Corporation of New York grant to the Sociolinguistics Program of the Center for Applied Linguistics.

ix

The sociolinguistic description is based on the correlation of linguistic and social variables. Although I have
attempted to keep technical linguistic terms to a minimum
and deliberately avoided the algebraic formulation of linguistic rules, it would be presumptuous for me to suggest
that this volume is intended for the non-linguist. Rather,
it is intended as a sociolinguistic case study for the person who has had some linguistic orientation. Particularly
in following the arguments on the structural composition of
Nonstandard Negro English, a knowledge of the theoretical
bases underlying linguistic analysis is assumed.

Somewhat apologetically, I have used the term "Nonstandard Negro English" to refer to the linguistic system
of working-class Negroes. In other publications, I have
used the term "Black English", first suggested to me by my
colleague Ralph W. Fasold. Although the two terms are
synonymous in their referential meaning, the term "Black
English" does not have the emotive overtones that Nonstandard
Negro English has, and is therefore preferable in view of the
current emphasis on racial pride in the black community. At
this stage, however, the term "Black English" has had only
limited public exposure, so that I have chosen to use the
more conventional term.

I am indebted to many people for their unselfish assistance during the development of this study. Roger W. Shuy,
director of the Sociolinguistics Program at the Center for
Applied Linguistics, has provided the opportunity for the
research which has resulted in this volume. Since my first
linguistics course as an undergraduate, he has been a consistent source of encouragement, the single most important
influence in directing my attention to the role of language
in society. Many discussions with my colleagues at the
Center for Applied Linguistics have made me consider issues

I would not have considered independently. The influence of Ralph W. Fasold is found in practically every part of the analysis, since he has been a constant sounding board for emerging ideas. William A. Stewart has made a number of significant observations on the structure of Nonstandard Negro English, and Joan C. Baratz has assisted in the research design for this study. Technical assistance was also provided by Judith L. Dobbins, Wesley F. Richardson, Carolyn H. Cunningham, Addie A. Allen, and Mary Jo Moore. Frank A. Rice has provided invaluable editorial assistance, and drawn the graphs. To Freda Ahearn I am indebted for her careful typing of the final manuscript.

Many individuals outside the Center for Applied Linguistics have also taken an interest in this study. William A. Samarin of the University of Toronto has guided my interest in sociolinguistics and carefully read the manuscript, making many important suggestions. J. Maurice Hohlfeld, Robert E. Cromack, and Robert C. Batchelder, all of the Hartford Seminary Foundation, have also made important suggestions on content and style, while Joan Rubin, of the University of Hawaii, gave considerable assistance in the early stages of this project. As in any current sociolinguistic research, my indebtedness to William Labov of Columbia University should be evident from the references in the text. He also read and commented on the manuscript. Finally, but most importantly, I am indebted to my wife. In addition to technical assistance in typing and proofreading, she has provided stability and optimism, without which this study would never have been completed. It is therefore that I dedicate this study to my wife, Marge.

W.A.W.
Washington, D.C.
May 1969

CONTENTS

1 INTRODUCTION

1.1 General Remarks

Within the last half century the populations of many large
Northern urban areas in the United States have been drastically restructured. Extensive in-migration by Southern
Negroes to Northern cities has resulted in the growth of
many, large, relatively isolated Negro communities. The
speech patterns in some of these communities differ greatly
from the existing speech patterns of the white community.
It has been noted, however, that within the Negro population
there is a considerable range of differences between speakers,
i.e. from those whose speech approximates the local variety
of standard English[1] to those who speak a variety sometimes
referred to as "Nonstandard Negro English" (Loflin 1967a).

   Although some attention has now been given to the most
nonstandard variety of speech in large urban areas (see sec.
1.3.2), the differences which exist among members of the Negro
population have been relatively neglected. These differences
are generally dismissed by statements such as "of course, not
all members of an urban Negro community are speakers of a
nonstandard dialect" (Stewart 1964b: 12). Several reasons
can be cited for the failure to study the speech of Negroes
from different socio-economic classes. In the first place,
speakers of a nonstandard variety of English appear to be
much more numerous than the speakers of a standard variety
of English in large metropolitan centers. Further, the

1

structural contrast between the local variety of standard
English and coexisting nonstandard dialect is unique to the
nonstandard speaker. Finally, the functional conflict between the socially prestigious standard English norm and the
socially stigmatized nonstandard English pattern has been the
focus of most concern.

It is becoming increasingly apparent that there is a
need to study the speech of a wider representation of American Negroes. To determine if speech is an indicator of social status in the Negro community it is necessary to study
the speech of Negroes from several different socio-economic
levels. A realistic approach to the speech of Negroes cannot
be satisfied with describing one restricted subset of that
community. Also, in order to understand the role of linguistic behavior in social mobility it is necessary to determine
how different linguistic variables correlate with certain
social characteristics. Finally, as a guide to educators
attempting to teach standard English it is essential to have
some understanding of what particular linguistic features
characterize specific socio-economic groups.

The speech of Negroes from several different socio-
economic levels is described in this study by focusing on
one Northern metropolitan area, the city of Detroit. In
many respects, Detroit can be considered as typical of other
large industrial cities in the North which have attracted
large numbers of Southern Negro in-migrants in the last 50
years. Although particular details of analysis may vary
from city to city, it is expected that the social stratification of the speech of Negroes in Detroit is representative
of other large Northern metropolitan areas.

1.2 Purpose

Ideally, one may think of the speech of Negroes in Detroit

in terms of two polar dialects--a socially superordinate
standard variety of English (referred to by Stewart [1964b:
15] as "acrolect") and a socially subordinate nonstandard
variety (referred to as "basilect").[2] Between these two
poles are a number of dialect strata characterized by variation between standard and nonstandard norms. The primary
focus of this study is the description of the variation between these two norms. The basic sociolinguistic method is
that of correlating social with linguistic variables. In
order to describe the correlation of social and linguistic
variables in the speech of Detroit Negroes, a number of
phonological and grammatical variables (see sec. 3.4) are
isolated and correlated with several different social variables.[3] The social variables include: (1) Social Status:
By dividing the population in terms of relative social status
the social distribution of particular linguistic features is
observed. (2) Racial Isolation: The amount of interaction
with the white community through peer group, school or work,
and neighborhood contacts is considered as a factor affecting the linguistic behavior of the Negro population. (3)
Age: Because the awareness of the social consequences of
speech is an acquired behavioral phenomenon, age is viewed
as an essential variable which intersects with other variables to account for differences in speech. (4) Sex: Different behavioral roles for men and women suggest that sex
may also intersect with other social variables to account
for differences in speech behavior. (5) Style: Formal differences in discourse types are also considered as a significant variable which may affect speech behavior. Although a
number of different styles might be delimited, in this study
only interview and reading styles are compared.

    In addition to the correlation of linguistic with social
variables, this study investigates the different relations

that socially diagnostic linguistic features may have to one
another. Specifically, we shall observe: (1) the extent to
which the social differentiation of linguistic variables is
quantitative or qualitative; (2) the relation between socially diagnostic phonological and grammatical variables;
and (3) the effect of independent linguistic constraints on
variability.

Although it is not the primary task of this study to
give a linguistic description of either the standard or nonstandard norms, a clear structural understanding of particular features in terms of these norms will be necessary. The
theoretical model of language underlying structural descriptions will be that of Stratificational Grammar (see Lamb 1964,
1966a, 1966b; Gleason 1964; Taber 1966).[4] The essential
aspect of Stratificational Grammar is its recognition of language organization on at least three Strata (semology, grammar, phonology). Each of the Strata has its own inventory
of units and tactics, being related to adjacent Strata only
through realization rules. Since the structural description
of features is secondary to their social stratification, no
formulaic representation of features will be given as a part
of this study.

1.3 Previous Studies

The merging of two areas in sociolinguistics has given rise
to this study. On the one hand, there is the development of
the systematic correlation of linguistic variables with social
differences. On the other hand, there is the systematic
treatment of Nonstandard Negro English as a self-contained
linguistic system apart from standard English. The development of these areas of sociolinguistics is discussed below.

1.3.1 The Social Stratification of Linguistic Variables

It is from the field of dialectology that the earliest modern attempts to account for social variation in speech can be cited. American dialectologists recognized that social differences had to be considered even though the primary goal of dialect geography was the correlation of settlement history with regional varieties of English. Kurath, for example, in directing the Linguistic Atlas of the United States and Canada, was aware that social differences intersected with settlement history and geographical difference to account for linguistic variation. As reported in the Handbook of the Linguistic Geography of New England, Linguistic Atlas fieldworkers divided informants into three main types, as follows:

Type I: Little formal education, little reading and restricted social contacts.

Type II: Better formal education (usually high school) and/or wider reading and social contacts.

Type III: Superior education (usually college), cultured background, wide reading and/or extensive social contacts (Kurath 1939: 44).

In addition, each of the above types was subdivided as:

Type A: Aged, and/or regarded by the fieldworker as old-fashioned.

Type B: Middle-aged or younger, and/or regarded by the fieldworker as more modern (Kurath 1939: 44).

Although different social types were recognized in the work of the Linguistic Atlas, several difficulties were apparent because the social parameter was not adequately considered. The social classification of informants was dependent on the fieldworkers' subjective impressions. The vagueness with which the social types were profiled (e.g. "little reading and restricted social contacts") caused the social classification of informants to be unreliable. Furthermore,

no verifiable sociological model for rating the social status
of informants was utilized. Education, which seemed to be
primary in the evaluation of informants, is only one of the
various factors which is used by social scientists in rating
social status.

   Whereas the correlation of social with linguistic differences was of secondary concern in the work of the Linguistic Atlas (Kurath 1941, 1949), later interpretation of the
Linguistic Atlas data gave more direct attention to the
importance of social factors in accounting for linguistic
diversity. Dialectologists, however, still seemed to appeal
to the social parameter only when "data proved too compli-
cated to be explained by merely a geographical statement or
a statement of settlement history" (McDavid 1948: 194).
Thus, McDavid's "Postvocalic -r in South Carolina: A Social
Analysis" (1948) amends a geographical explanation of post-
vocalic -r in the Piedmont area of South Carolina by analyzing
the intersection of social class with geographical differences.
A recent treatment of the social parameter in describing a
speech community by a dialectologist can be found in Pederson's
(1965) description of English phonology in Chicago.

   From a differing viewpoint, anthropologists have made
significant contributions to the study of linguistic correlates of social stratification in the last decade. Whereas
dialectologists have been satisfied with rough approximations
of social divisions to which linguistic phenomena may be related, anthropologists have characteristically been rigorous
in their differentiation of social groups to which linguistic
variables may be related. Independent ethnographical description of behavioral patterns characterizing different social
strata is required before any correlation of linguistic variables with these strata can be made. Research on the social
stratification of linguistic features has been pioneered by

Gumperz (1958a, 1958b, 1961, 1964), Hymes (1961, 1964), and Bright (1960, 1964, 1966). For example, Gumperz, in several articles (1958a, 1958b), has shown how linguistic variables, particularly phonological variables, relate to the caste systems of India. Southeastern Asia, perhaps because of its rigid stratification between castes, has received the most extensive consideration by anthropologists. Anthropological linguists such as Hymes (1961, 1964) and Ervin-Tripp (1964) have concerned themselves with developing a structural taxonomy of the factors which must be dealt with from a sociolinguistic perspective of verbal behavior. For example, Ervin-Tripp (1964) suggests that settings, participants, topics, and functions of interaction all must be considered from a sociolinguistic perspective of speech. Little consideration has been given to American English by anthropologists, although Fisher (1958) provided an analysis of the morphemic variation between the suffixal participle /-ɪn/ and /-ɪŋ/ in English by considering the social background of 24 children in a New England town.

The contributions of sociologists to the social stratification of linguistic variables, until recently, have been minimal. Labov (1966a: 23) notes that "psychologists and sociologists have lacked the linguistic training required to isolate particular elements of language structure, and have worked primarily with vocabulary or content analysis." Sociologists have made their most significant contribution in demanding valid methods of research design and sampling. Pickford (1956), for example, notes the errors of "reliability" and "validity" which characterize the work of the Linguistic Atlas. Research design and sampling techniques in current sociolinguistic work have profited mainly from the insights of sociologists. Recent interest by sociologists in the linguistic parameter is evidenced by a volume

of Sociological Inquiry (1966) dedicated to explorations in
sociolinguistics. The research of Bernstein (1960, 1961,
1964, 1966) and Levine and Crockett (1966, 1967) is relevant
to current work on the social stratification of linguistic
variables.

It was Labov's work on the social stratification of
English in New York City (1964a, 1964b, 1965, 1966a, 1966b,
1966c) more than any other research, that combined the insights of linguistics and sociology. Using a survey by the
Mobilization for Youth as his sociological model, he analyzed
the speech of over a hundred, randomly selected informants.
Five different phonological variables (oh, eh, r, th, dh),
isolated in four contextual styles (careful speech, casual
speech, reading, word lists) were correlated with the social
stratification of the informants. Labov made several major
contributions to the study of linguistic correlates of social
stratification. In the first place, he used sociologically
valid procedures in selecting the informants for his sample.
Many linguists prior to Labov were largely satisfied with
biased, non-random informant selection. Also, Labov's
quantitative measurement of linguistic variables, although
not the first, was considerably more extensive than any previous sociolinguistic research. Further, his effort to isolate contextual styles on the basis of extra-linguistic
"channel cues" was a careful attempt to define interview
styles in linguistics. The major contribution of Labov was
his demonstration that speech differences within a community,
often dismissed by linguists as "free variation", systematically correlated with social differences.

The Detroit Dialect Study (Shuy, Wolfram and Riley 1967),
from which the corpus for the present research is taken,
experimented with several different methods of analyzing
speech differences. It extended the insights of Labov on the

linguistic variable to grammatical as well as phonological variables. An attempt to measure differences by the quantitative measurement of structural types (e.g. clause and phrase types) was also investigated.

The present study enlarges the sociolinguistic description of Detroit speech in several ways. Based on preliminary research by Shuy, Wolfram and Riley (1967), it expands the correlation of linguistic and social variables. Only two grammatical variables (multiple negation and pronominal apposition) and one phonological variable (syllable-final nasal) were investigated in the original study. This study expands the investigation to four phonological and four grammatical variables. In addition, it investigates the relationship between socially diagnostic phonological and grammatical variables. Furthermore, the selection of linguistic variables in the original study was restricted to those which were socially diagnostic for both the Negro and white community. In this study, several variables which are applicable only to the Negro community are investigated. Finally, the selection of informants in this study is more rigid than the original study. Informants for the preliminary study were disproportionately distributed in the different social classes. This meant that several social classes were not adequately represented. But this study is designed so that informants are evenly distributed in each of the four social classes represented (see sec. 1.4.1).

1.3.2   The Systematic Study of Nonstandard Negro English

Although the speech of American Negroes has frequently been represented in folk literature, until recently it has received little attention from linguists. On the one hand, this lack of attention can be attributed to the attitude that nonstandard speech is less worthy of interest than the

study of socially acceptable varieties of English. On the
other hand, the disregard for nonstandard Negro English is
due to the fact that scholars of the English language have
generally assumed the identity of Negro and uneducated white
Southern speech.

For the most part, it was dialectologists who concluded
that nonstandard Negro English was not essentially different
from the speech of Southern whites of comparable socio-
economic levels. Thus Kurath, in A Word Geography of the
Eastern United States (1949: 6), notes:

> By and large the Southern Negro speaks the language of
> the white man of his locality or area and of his edu-
> cation.... As far as the speech of the uneducated
> Negroes is concerned, it differs little from that of
> the illiterate white; that is, it exhibits the same
> regional and local variations as that of the simple
> white folk.

Raven I. McDavid, presently an influential American
dialectologist, has reinforced Kurath's position:

> With our current knowledge it is safest to assume that
> in general the range of variants is the same in Negro
> and in white speech, though the statistical distribu-
> tion of variants has been skewed by the American caste
> system (1965: 258).

Even studies conducted only with Negro informants assumed
the same position. Juanita Williamson, in A Phonological and
Morphological Study of the Speech of the Negro of Memphis,
Tennessee (1961: 1) maintains:

> It is generally recognized by linguists that the speech
> of the Negro is not a "distinct entity" and does not
> differ materially from that of the whites of the same
> economic and educational level of the area in which he
> has lived the greater part of his life.

One exception to the identity of white Southern and Negro
dialects has been recognized by dialectologists, namely,
Gullah or Geechee, spoken along the coasts of South Carolina
and Georgia. Gullah is generally considered to be an English-

based creole, even by dialectologists (McDavid and McDavid
1951: 6). Dialectologists have considered this creole to be
an anomaly among other nonstandard Negro dialects (McDavid
1963: 476).

The recognition that Negro dialects other than Gullah
must be considered systematically different from white dialects can be largely attributed to the work of such creole
specialists as Stewart (1964a, 1964b, 1967, 1968), Dillard
(1967, 1968), and Bailey (1965, 1968). These have maintained
that present-day Negro dialects are derived, not from British
dialects as dialectologists have assumed, but from a creole
variety of English which was spoken by the earliest slaves.[5]
Stewart notes:

> Of those Africans who fell victim to the Atlantic slave
> trade and were brought to the New World, many found it
> necessary to learn some kind of English. With very few
> exceptions, the form of English which they acquired was
> a pidginized one, and this kind of English became so
> well-established as the principal medium of communica-
> tion between Negro slaves in the British colonies that
> it was passed on as a creole language to succeeding
> generations of the New World Negroes, for whom it was
> their native tongue (1967: 22).

Present-day Negro dialect has resulted from a process
which Stewart labels "decreolization" (i.e. the loss of
creole features). Through contact with the British-derived
dialects the creole variety of English spoken by Negroes
merged with other dialects of English. The merging process,
however, was neither instantaneous nor complete. Stewart
asserts:

> Indeed, the non-standard speech of present-day American
> Negroes still seems to exhibit structural traces of a
> creole predecessor, and this is probably a reason why
> it is in some ways more deviant from standard English
> than is the non-standard speech of even the most un-
> educated American whites (1968: 3).

Stewart substantiates his claim that Negro dialects

derived from a widespread slave creole by examining the close
relationship which is found between 18th and 19th century
Negro dialect and other New World creoles (Stewart 1967).

The above discussion clearly indicates that the creolist
perspective on Negro dialect has come into sharp conflict
with dialectology's traditional view of white Southern and
Negro dialect differences. What then, can account for this
sharp difference of opinion? One explanation is that dialectologists have focused their attention on the similarities
between nonstandard Negro dialects and white dialects, whereas
creolists have focused on the differences between these two
varieties of English. Dialectologists have been largely
occupied with phonological and lexical differences, the levels
on which the dialects are nearly (but not completely) alike.
Creolists, on the other hand, have concerned themselves with
subtle differences between grammatical categories. The most
serious consequence of the creolist position seems to be
that many of the differences between the dialects are viewed
as "deep structure" differences.[6] Thus, Bailey, in "Toward
a New Perspective in Negro English Dialectology" (1965a: 172)
remarks:

> I would like to suggest that the Southern Negro "dialect"
> differs from other Southern speech because its deep
> structure is different, having its origins as it un-
> doubtedly does in some Proto-Creole grammatical struc-
> ture.

At this point in the research of Nonstandard Negro
English (henceforth abbreviated NNE), the question of the
historical relationship between NNE and white dialects has
not been satisfactorily answered. Only additional investigation of NNE as a system in itself and as a system which
shows both similarities and differences with other varieties
of English will resolve the controversy.

Linguists not accepting the creolist historical

interpretation (or, as descriptivists, uninterested in the historical derivation of NNE) have now taken up the systematic description of Negro dialects. Views concerning the significance of the differences between NNE and white dialects vary drastically. Loflin, for example, maintains that:

> Efforts to construct a grammar for Nonstandard Negro English suggest that the similarities between it and Standard English are superficial. There is every reason, at this stage of research to believe that a fuller description of Nonstandard Negro English will show a grammatical system which must be treated as a foreign language (1967a: 1312).

Other linguists have recognized systematic differences between white and Negro dialects, but have seen the differences to be of minor rather than major significance. Labov and Cohen suggest:

> ...The general indication of our work so far is that the differences between this dialect and standard English are greater on the surface than in the underlying grammatical structure (1967: 66).

Still others, such as Fasold (forthcoming), have taken a moderate view:

> Since we are dealing with two dialects of the same language, it seems likely that the differences we find will be relatively small ones. However, this by no means implies that they are of little consequence. Some of these differences involve the deepest level of language, that of possible message. In other words, it can be shown that there are messages possible in Black English which are not possible in Standard English and vice-versa.

The views of Labov, Loflin, and Fasold indicate the wide range of opinions held concerning the significance of the differences between NNE and white dialects. Nevertheless, these scholars essentially agree (and in this they unite with the creolists) in their insistence that systematic differences must be recognized between the NNE and other varieties of English.

Since systematic differences between NNE and other dialects of English have only been recognized in the last several years, there are few available descriptions of NNE.
Loflin, in several articles (1967a, 1967b), has focused on
the verb system, maintaining the dominance of aspect over
tense and the unique nature of be copula in NNE. Somewhat
differing interpretations of be have been offered by Fasold
(forthcoming), Feigenbaum (forthcoming) and Labov, et al.
(1968). Labov, et al. (1965a, 1967, 1968) have done preliminary analysis of both grammar and phonology, with emphasis on the latter. Recently, Labov (1968) has suggested that
the absence of the copula (e.g. he nice 'he is nice') can be
accounted for by extending the contraction rules of Standard
English (henceforth abbreviated as SE) to cover what he considers "deletion" of copula in NNE. Meanwhile, Loman (1967a)
has studied intonation and made available a series of texts
for analysis (1967b).

Currently, the most concentrated research on NNE is being conducted in New York City by William Labov and asso-
ciates (1965, 1968) and in Washington, D.C. by the staff of
the Sociolinguistics Program under the direction of Roger W.
Shuy at the Center for Applied Linguistics. The present
study expands research on the structure of NNE in two ways.
First, several NNE features which have not been investigated
previously are described. Second, it serves as a basis for
comparing the structure of NNE in several different cities.

1.4 Corpus

1.4.1 Sample

This study is based on the speech of 48 Negro informants,
chosen from a random sample of over 700 interviews on file
with the Detroit Dialect Study.[7] These interviews were conducted mainly during the summer of 1966[8] under the direction

of Dr. Roger W. Shuy, formerly of Michigan State University
and presently director of the Sociolinguistics Program at
the Center for Applied Linguistics. The informants are evenly
distributed among four social classes referred to here as
upper-middle, lower-middle, upper-working, and lower-working
class (see sec. 2.3). Within each social group four informants from each of three age groups were selected: 10-to-
12-year-old pre-adolescents, 14-to-17-year-old teen-agers,
and 30-to-55-year-old adults. The 10-to-12-year-old pre-
adolescents were chosen to represent a stage at which language acquisition is no longer a factor but conscious awareness of the social consequences of linguistic behavior is
minimal. The teen-agers represent a stage at which there
is an increasing awareness of social consequences of speech.
Adults represent the stage at which a fully developed set of
values toward speech behavior can be expected (see Labov
1964b). Both sexes are equally represented in the sample.

In addition to the 48 Negro informants, 12 upper-middle
class white informants have been selected, divided equally
by age and sex. White informants were included only in order
to compare the speech of those Negroes most closely approximating SE with whites of an equal social class (for a complete list of informants, see Appendix A).

Informants for this study were selected from the full
Detroit corpus on the basis of the following criteria:

(1)   The informant should be a resident of Detroit for at
      least ten years. Preferably, adults should have lived
      in Detroit half their life. All children and teen-
      agers should be native Detroiters.[9]

(2)   The recording fidelity of the tape should be adequate
      for phonetic transcription.

(3)   There should be a sufficient amount of discourse to
      expect a reasonable variety of syntactic structures.

Although the above criteria somewhat restrict the ran-
domness of the sample, this type of restriction appears
necessary for a linguistic study of this type.

1.4.2   The Interview

Each informant was interviewed with a standardized questionnaire (see Appendix B).[10] Generally, the interviews, lasting
approximately an hour, were tape-recorded in the home of the
informant. The same questionnaire, with appropriate adaptation, was used for all ages and social levels. It was designed
to elicit spontaneous conversation, single item responses, and
reading style. In the conversation sections, topics ranging
from childhood games to fate were discussed in an attempt to
elicit connected discourse. Stringent uniformity was sacri-
ficed for the sake of eliciting extended discourse. Generally,
topics in which informants evidenced interest were pursued by
the interviewer. The conversation section, which is of primary interest in this study, lasted from 30 to 45 minutes.

As in any interview situation, there were certain
restrictions on the spontaneity of the conversation. These
resulted from the presence of the tape recorder, the difference in the race of the interviewer and informant, and the
unnaturalness of the interview situation. In order to alle-
viate some of the uncomfortableness inherent in the interview situation several methods were used. First, lavaliere
microphones were used so that the presence of a microphone
was not within immediate observation. The discussion of
familiar events, such as games, movies, pets, etc., also
caused the informant to become involved in the descriptions
of a particular event or object, easing some of the formality
of the interview situation. Furthermore, conducting the
interview in a familiar environment, such as the home, helped
reduce some of the suspicion associated with the interview.

Finally, and perhaps most importantly, fieldworkers attempted to create an informal atmosphere for the interview.

No effort was made to conceal the fact that we were interested in how different people in Detroit spoke, although details about the specific focus of the study, the correlation of linguistic with social variables, was generally unknown to the informants. In many instances, the fieldworker's concern about speech was interpreted by the informants as an interest in how different people recite rhymes, tell stories, discuss events, and refer to particular objects.

According to Shuy, Wolfram and Riley (1968: 28), the recorded speech elicited in the Detroit Dialect Study interview was not quite casual but not quite formal. It seemed to be a good sample of the speech used by children to adults and adults to respected strangers. Rarely can it be considered in-group speech. Rather than a disadvantage, for the purposes of this study, the elicitation of this type of speech may be viewed as an advantage since it is one of the most important styles of speech used by Americans. Shuy, Wolfram and Riley (1968: 28) observe that it is the style in which Americans make their moves up (or down) the social scale.

NOTES

1. Standard English is defined in this study as a socially acceptable variety of English established by a codified norm of "correctness". Nonstandard English is defined as any variety of English which differs from this established norm.

2. Originally, some features of the nonstandard variety of Negro English may have been an acceptable regional pattern (i.e. a Southern dialect). What we have seen in many large Northern cities is the transformation of a regional dialect into a class and ethnic pattern. McDavid

(1967: 27) notes that this type of transformation is
quite common in language history.

3. The isolation of social variables in this study is not
    meant to imply that these are the only significant social
    variables which might have been isolated. For example,
    one significant variable might have been the informant's
    length of residency in Detroit. Since the focus of the
    study is the current social stratification of the speech
    of Negroes in Detroit, only informants who had been
    long-time residents (see sec. 1.4.1) of Detroit were
    chosen so that the speech patterns would be determined
    primarily by social contacts in Detroit.

4. Unfortunately, the separate terminological conventions
    of sociology and linguistics have resulted in the use of
    stratification and strata in two distinct senses: (1) as
    a technical term associated with a particular theoretical
    model of language description recognizing several dis-
    tinct levels of language organization, and (2) as a tech-
    nical term associated with a socio-economic level of
    society. In order not to confuse these two senses,
    stratification and strata will be capitalized when re-
    ferring to the model of language description.

5. Prior to creolist interpretations, there had been occa-
    sional reference to the existence of qualitative differ-
    ences between Southern white and Negro nonstandard
    features. For example, Wise (1957: 297-302) distin-
    guishes "specific features of substandard Southern Negro
    speech" from "features of substandard Negro speech held
    in common with substandard Southern white speech".

6. "Deep structure" has been used traditionally to refer to
    the "base component" in a transformational-generative
    view of language. From the viewpoint of Stratificational
    grammar, it is interpreted to refer to the lexemic Stra-
    tum (see Taber 1966: 63).

7. Tapes of the interviews are now on file at the Center for
    Applied Linguistics in Washington, D.C.

8. Since the original sample inadequately represented the
    upper-middle class Negro population, more interviews were
    conducted by the writer in the fall of 1967 to obtain an
    adequate sample of the Negro middle class.

9. Although it might have been preferable to restrict adult
    informants to lifetime residents of Detroit, the random

sample did not produce a sufficient number of informants
to meet this condition. In-migration is clearly the
rule rather than the exception among the adult Negro
population.

10. For a fuller description and evaluation of the interview,
see Shuy, Wolfram and Riley, Field Techniques in an Urban
Language Study (1968).

2 THE SOCIAL SETTING FOR LINGUISTIC DIVERSITY

The relevant historical and sociological context of the Negro population provides a background for understanding the speech behavior of Negroes in Detroit. Three essential factors to be considered in any treatment of the speech of Detroit Negroes are: (1) the trends of in-migration which have resulted in the drastic restructuring of the racial distribution of Detroit; (2) the role of racial isolation as a factor influencing linguistic behavior; and (3) the role of social status in accounting for speech differences within the community.

2.1 Patterns of In-migration

Since World War I, Detroit, like many other large Northern metropolitan areas, has undergone drastic changes in its racial distribution. The growing inadequacy of employment opportunities in Southern agriculture, coupled with the opportunities for unskilled workers at rising rates of pay in the Northern industrial cities, has prompted large numbers of Negroes to leave the South during the past half century. Detroit became known for its heavy industry and high wages during this period, a fact which no doubt encouraged large numbers of migrant Negroes searching for economic opportunity to settle in this area (Lenski 1961: 33).

From a total of 5,741 Negroes reported in the 1910 Census, the figure has grown to an estimated 600,000, or

approximately 37 per cent of the Detroit population in 1967.
Essentially, there have been two major waves of migration,
separated by a decade of relatively low mobility during the
depression period. Between 1910 and 1930 the Negro population increased by over 100,000; between 1940 and 1960 by
over 300,000. During the first wave of Negro in-migrants,
the growth of the white population, although not as drastic
as that of the Negro, was steady. In the past 20 years this
trend has changed, largely due to the exodus of the white
population to the suburbs. Thus, in less than 20 years the
city has lost about 200,000 people but the Negro population
has shown a gain of about 300,000. During the 1950s and 60s
the trend of Negro in-migration has leveled off somewhat.
Sharp (1960: 2) notes that the Negro population grew six
times faster than the white population between 1940-1950,
but only three times as fast between 1950-1960.

The resultant pattern of distribution of the Detroit
Negro population indicates that the vast majority of the
adult population consists of non-native Detroiters. On the
other hand, increasing numbers of children and teen-agers
have resided in Detroit all their lives. Although the proportion of Negroes who are lifetime residents of Detroit is
steadily rising, the percentage of Negroes born in the Detroit
area is still considerably lower than that of the white population at all age levels. Fig. 1 shows the contrast between
the percentage of Negroes and whites born in the state of
Michigan for age levels ranging from 10-49. The figures are
based on information available in the United States Census
of Population: 1960, Michigan.[1]

In Fig. 1, the curve for the white population reveals
a rather steady decline, dropping from 83 per cent (in the
10-14 age level) to 41 per cent (in the 45-49 age level, an
overall decline of 42 per cent. The curve for the Negro

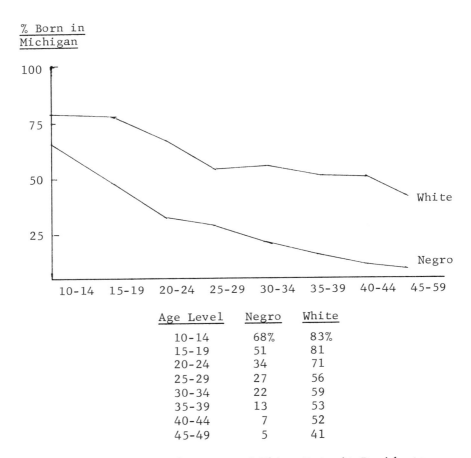

Fig. 1.   Percentage of Negro and White Detroit Residents
          Born in Michigan: By Age Levels

population shows a decline of 63 per cent (from 68 to 5 per
cent), and reveals a sharper decline between the adults
(over 20) and children and teen-agers (under 20) than the
white curve. For example, between the ages of 10-14 and
20-24 there is a decline of 34 per cent in the Negro curve.
For the white, the decline between these ages is only 12 per
cent. The sharp curve for the Negro population represents
the gradual leveling off of Negro in-migrants since 1950.
Because of the increasing numbers of Negroes being born in
the Detroit area, the speech of Negro residents can no longer

be dismissed simply as the retention of a regional speech
variety (i.e. a Southern dialect) after migrating to Detroit.
Rather, it must be viewed as an ethnic and class pattern.

Having observed the rapid settlement of vast numbers of
Negroes in Detroit, we now turn to the Southern origin of
this population. In Fig. 2 the state of birth for Negro
residents is given, based on the <u>United States Census of</u>
<u>Population: 1960, Mobility for States and Economic Areas</u>.
Percentages are given for states which account for one or
more per cent of Detroit Negro residents.

Fig.2.   Negro Residents of Michigan: By State of Birth

In Fig. 2, it is necessary to interpret the high percentage of Negro residents born in Michigan in relation to
Fig. 1, which showed that the vast majority of Negroes born
in the area were children and teen-agers. The relatively high
percentage of Negroes born in Michigan can be accounted for
by the fact that the census figures on mobility make no differentiation between various age levels. Despite this defic-
iency, a fairly clear pattern emerges. The Detroit Negro
population is largely drawn from the South Central states,
primarily Alabama, Mississippi, and Georgia. The particular
Southern origin of the Detroit Negro appears to contrast
with the in-migration patterns of Eastern cities such as
Philadelphia, New York and Washington, D.C., which draw the
majority of their in-migrants from the South Atlantic coastal
region, including South Carolina, North Carolina, and the
Georgia coast.[2] William A. Stewart (personal communication)
suggests that some differences in the NNE of Negroes in
various Northern cities can be traced to different Southern
origins.

At this point, one may ask if the sample chosen for this
study represents the overall figures of Southern origin for
the entire Detroit population. In Fig. 3, the birthplace of
the parents for the 48 Negro informants is tabulated. The
percentage of parents from each state is given for all states
accounting for more than 2 per cent of the sample. The figures seem to be representative of the overall Negro population in that the same general pattern of migration from the
South Central States is observed. Over 50 per cent of the
informants' parents are from the states of Alabama, Georgia
and Mississippi.

The fact that Detroit Negroes show a consistent pattern
of Southern origin does not in itself, of course, account
for the particular type of linguistic behavior manifested by

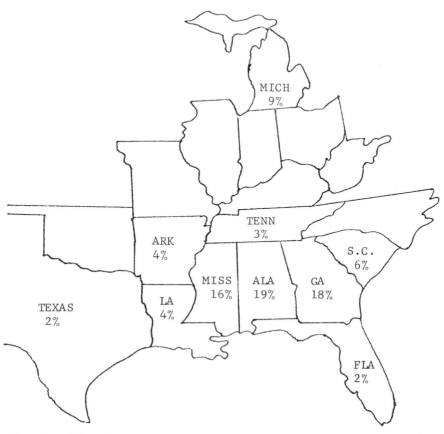

Fig. 3. Distribution of Birthplaces of Informants'
         Parents: By State of Birth

Detroit Negroes. The roles of racial isolation and class differences, among others, must also be considered as essential
background factors for examining their linguistic behavior.

2.2 Racial Isolation

One of the most important factors accounting for speech behavior in the Detroit Negro population is racial isolation.
Patterns of Northern segregation are a main source for trans-
forming many Southern speech characteristics into ethnic and
class patterns of speech in Northern cities. In order to

understand the role of racial isolation as a variable affecting speech behavior three factors can be mentioned:
(1) residential; (2) educational; and (3) peer group isolation. These will be discussed briefly for the general
population and more specifically in relation to the informants used in this study.

2.2.1 Residential Isolation

Like many other Northern cities in which relatively isolated
Negro communities have arisen, the Negro population of Detroit
has been most heavily concentrated in the inner or central
city area (see Racial Isolation in the Public Schools 1967:
11-13). In order to show this concentration of the Detroit
Negro population one may divide the city into a number of
different areas which have emerged as spontaneous and un-
planned by-products of the growth of the metropolis (Lenski
1962: 76). Lenski (1961: 76-79) has divided the metropolitan area into Inner City, Middle City, and Outer City
(see Fig. 4). Inner City and Middle City are divided into
East and West Sections on the basis of the main east-west
division in Detroit, Woodward Avenue. Outer City is divided
into East, Central, and West Sections. Also included are
the municipalities of Hamtramck and Highland Park, which are
totally surrounded by the muncipality of Detroit. In Fig. 4
the percentage of Negroes in each of these sections is given,
based on United States Census of Population and Housing: 1960,
Detroit, Michigan.[3] The map reveals the concentration of
Negroes in the Inner and Middle City areas, Inner City East
having the most heavily concentrated Negro population (75 per
cent). Since the 1960 census, it appears that Outer City
Central has proportionately increased its Negro population
the most, attracting many middle-class Negroes as the middle-
class white population continues its exodus from this area.

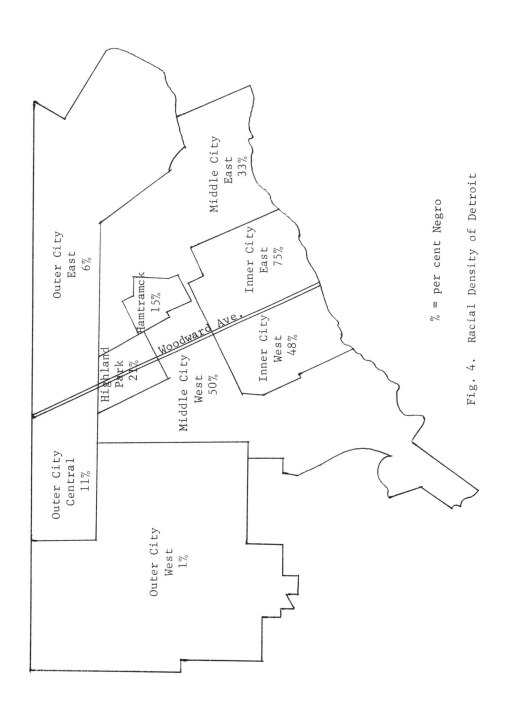

Outer City
East
6%

Middle City
East
33%

Outer City
Central
11%

Hamtramck
15%

Highland
Park
27%

Inner City
East
75%

Woodward Ave.

Middle City
West
50%

Inner City
West
48%

Outer City
West
1%

% = per cent Negro

Fig. 4. Racial Density of Detroit

Since the relative isolation in residency may be considered as a potential factor affecting the speech behavior
of the informants used in this study, the percentage of
Negroes in each census tract where informants lived has been
tabulated. Five main categories are distinguished: (1) Negro
(90-100 per cent Negro); (2) predominately Negro (60-89 per
cent Negro); (3) mixed (40-59 per cent Negro); (4) predominantly white (10-39 per cent Negro); and (5) white (0-9 per
cent Negro). The distribution of informants in terms of these
categories is summarized in Table 1.

Table 1

Racial Isolation of Informants: Residency

Residential Area[4]	No. of Informants
Negro	15
Predominantly Negro	27
Mixed	5
Predominantly White	1
White	0

The familiar pattern of residential segregation needs
little explanation. What is of concern in this study is the
potential influence mixed and predominantly white neighbor-
hoods might have on the speech of a small minority of informants. It can be hypothesized that Negro informants living in
mixed or predominantly white residential areas will reveal
speech patterns more closely approximating SE than those
living in segregated areas.

2.2.2 Educational Isolation

Closely related to the pattern of residential isolation is
the pattern of segregation in the schools for the children

and work for the adults. As of 1965, approximately 57 per
cent of all students in the Detroit public schools were
Negro. In 1965 more than 70 per cent of the Negro children
attended schools where there were 90-100 per cent Negroes
and over 90 per cent schools where a majority of the students
were Negroes (U.S. Commission on Civil Rights 1967: 7). The
following distribution, divided into categories on the basis
of the same percentages as the residential table (see Table 1),
obtains for the informants used in this study.[5]

Table 2
Racial Isolation of Informants: Schools Attended

School Area	No. of Informants
Negro	25
Predominantly Negro	10
Mixed	9
Predominantly White	4
White	0

We see in Table 2 that the great majority of informants
either attend or have attended Negro or predominantly Negro
schools. The importance of student norms for speech behavior (which, in most Negro schools, must be considered
NNE) was well illustrated by one upper-middle class female
teen-age informant who recounted her first experience in
public speaking at an exclusively Negro junior high school.
Her style of speech, a close approximation of SE, was ridi-
culed by the students as "talking like a white person" and
"trying to speak like a snob".

2.2.3 Peer Group Isolation
The role of peer group influence is probably the most important

aspect of racial isolation in terms of speech behavior. For
each informant in this study, an estimation of the amount of
interaction with white peers was made, based on Part III of
the questionnaire, which dealt with group structure (see
Appendix B). Answers to direct questions about racial isolation in peer groups (e.g. "Do you have any white people
you hang around with?") were checked with the personal data
on residential, school, or work integration, and other references made to peers in the course of the conversation (and
in several instances by direct observation of peers present
at the time of the interview). Ultimately, the categorization was subjective. The following are typical responses to
questions about peer group integration:

Informant No. 565

Fieldworker: Are there girls you like to hang around with?
Informant: Let me see.
Fieldworker: Just name them!
Informant: Gwendolyn, Gail, Brenda, Barbara, Christine,
               Wanda, Jennie, Nadine.
Fieldworker: Any of them white?
Informant: Nope...I know a white boy, he nice.

Informant No. 707

Fieldworker: Most of the kids you go around with, are they
               Negro or white, or both or what?
Informant: Well, I'd say the majority of the kids I play
               with are white, 'cause that's more of 'em live
               down here and, my favorite friends I'd say are
               the Joneses [fictitious name]...

It is apparent that Informant No. 565, although referring
to a white boy who is an acquaintance, should be classified
as having only Negro peers. This categorization is clearly
supported by the residential and educational classification
of the informant, which are predominantly Negro. Informant
No. 707 is classified as having predominantly white peers,
since his statement about peer group integration is supported
by mixed residential and educational ratings (and in this

case, direct observation of peers prior to and after the
interview).

Table 3 summarizes the distribution of informants on
the basis of peer group isolation.

Table 3

Racial Isolation of Informants: Peer Group

Peer Group	No. of Informants
Negro	25
Predominantly Negro	16
Mixed	5
Predominantly White	2
White	0

The significant division in Table 3 seems to be between
those informants having only Negro or predominantly Negro
peers (it is debatable whether or not some of those rated as
predominantly Negro should, in fact, be categorized as Negro)
and the seven informants rated as having mixed or predominantly white peers.

Although a quantitative index of racial isolation could
be constructed on the basis of the above three factors, it
has not been attempted in this study. Since residency,
school, and peer group seem to be so closely related, and
estimates of peer group (and for adults, work) integration
were ultimately subjective impressions of the writer, it
would be presumptuous to suggest a rigid classification.
Rather, racial isolation is referred to in this study inci-
dentally as it intersects with other social variables to
account for speech diversity.

2.3 Social Status

In a study that correlates linguistic performance with social
stratification, the relative social status must be measured
on the basis of some objective, nonlinguistic criteria. A
comprehensive independent sociological survey delimiting the
different socio-economic groups and the distinct behavioral
patterns characterizing each group should serve as a basis
for correlating the linguistic features with social status.
Unfortunately, no extensive socio-economic survey exists for
Detroit, although the Detroit Area Study of the University
of Michigan has related various kinds of social variation to
different socio-economic groups in Detroit (see The Detroit
Area Study 1960). It becomes the task of this study either
to devise its own or adopt some verifiable sociological model
for ranking informants on a socio-economic scale. Although
there are a number of available sociological models which
might be followed, the one used in this investigation is the
same as that used by the Detroit Dialect Study (see Shuy,
Wolfram and Riley 1967).[6]

This model, which is an adaptation of Hollinghead's
scale (1958), combines scales of education, occupation, and
residency in computing the relative social rank of informants.
Each score is computed for the head of the household. Table
4 presents the education scale. The occupation scale is presented in Table 5.

The residency scale (Table 6) is based primarily on the
percentage of adequately constructed houses with all plumbing
facilities and the average number (arithmetic mean) of rooms
per occupied unit in the census block where the informant
lives. This information is based on United States Housing:
1960, Detroit, Michigan. Appropriate adjustments are made
on the basis of median income in the census tract (no figures
for the blocks are available) and percentage of houses in the

Table 4

Education Scale

Rating	Level of Education
1	Any graduate degree
2	College education
3	One year or more of college
4	High school graduation
5	Some high school (tenth grade)
6	Junior high school
7	Less than seven years

Table 5

Occupation Scale

Rating	Occupation	Example of Occupation
1	Major professionals; executives of large concerns	Lawyers, doctors, divisional managers of large industrial enterprises
2	Lesser professionals; executives of medium-sized concerns	High school teachers, assistants to executives, real estate salesmen
3	Semi-professionals; administrators of small business	Auto salesmen, postal clerks, librarians
4	Technicians; owners of petty businesses	Factory foremen, stenographers, electricians (own business)
5	Skilled workmen	Carpenters, telephone linemen, policemen
6	Semi-skilled workmen	Gas station attendants, taxi-drivers, baggage men
7	Unskilled workers	Odd-job men, scrubwomen, heavy labor workers

block with more than 1.01 persons per room. Six residency
rankings are distinguished on the basis of the house condition and average number of rooms per occupied unit. The
following matrix, with the rating given in each cell, gives
the characteristics of each rank:

Table 6

Residency Scale

No. of Rooms Per Occupied Unit	Percentage of Sound Houses with all Plumbing Facilities				
	100.0	87.5-99.9	66.6-87.4	50.0-66.5	0-50.0
10.5+	1	1	2	3	4
7.5-10.4	1	2	3	4	5
5.5- 7.4	2	3	4	5	6
4.5- 5.4	3	4	5	6	6
1- 4.4	4	5	6	6	6

Each informant is given a 1-6 rating on the basis of
the above scale. Appropriate adjustments are then made on
the basis of median income and number of persons per room
for the census track. If the median family income for the
census tract is $2,000 higher or lower than "appropriate"
median income for any rank (as calculated by sociologists)
the rating is adjusted one level accordingly (i.e. either up
or down one rank). The six median income levels are presented in Table 7.

In addition to the appropriate adjustment for median
income, the rating is lowered one (unless the lowest rating,
6, had already been assigned) if over one-third of all occupied units in the census block had more than 1.01 persons
per room.

Table 7

Income Levels

Rating	Median	Range: Median Income
1	$14,220	$10,000 to $18,440
2	9,213	9,026 to 12,916
3	6,362	5,111 to 8,809
4	6,327	4,254 to 7,648
5	4,713	4,085 to 6,008
6	3,582	1,879 to 4,440

At this point, three ratings are given: (1) a rating of 1-7 for education; (2) a rating of 1-7 for occupation; and (3) a rating of 1-6 for residency. These figures are multiplied by factors of 5, 9, and 6, respectively, to determine the social status score.[7] The possible scores range from 20 (e.g. a doctor living in a block which is rated 1 on the residency scale) to 134 (e.g. an unskilled worker having less than 7 years of education and living in a block rated 6 on the residency scale). Thus, the lower the score, the higher the relative social status.

The above scale estimates social status differences in terms of a continuum of scores. For the purposes of this study, these scores are converted into a limited number of discrete social "classes".[8] Following preliminary studies by the Detroit Area Study (1966), four classes are delimited for the Detroit population and designated here as upper-middle, lower-middle, upper-working, and lower-working classes. These four groups are assigned on the basis of a mathematical breakdown of a social status score into quartiles (see Table 8).

In selecting the informants for this study, a discrepancy of at least 7 points is maintained between the highest score

Table 8

Social Status Scores for Four Social Classes

Class Designation	Social Status Scores
Upper-middle	20-48
Lower-middle	49-77
Upper-working	78-106
Lower-working	107-134

of a given level and lowest score of the next higher level
in order to minimize problems of marginality between groups.

The frequency distribution of the Detroit Negro population in terms of the four social classes designated here
differs from that of the white population, primarily because
of the greater restrictions in social mobility among Negroes.
Thus, when one describes the speech of the upper-middle and
lower-middle class Negroes, this represents a much smaller
(but not in any sense less important) segment of the Negro
population than if one were to describe the speech of the
white population in terms of the same groups. Fig. 5 shows
the distribution of white and Negro informants in the "base
sample" of the Detroit Dialect Study (see the Appendix:
"Detroit School Sample" in Shuy, Wolfram and Riley 1967).

Less than 15 per cent of all Negroes are found in the
upper two classes, whereas over 40 per cent of the white
population is found in these same classes. The description
of speech behavior for the upper- and lower-working classes
represents the vast majority of Negro speakers in Detroit.

After selecting 12 informants to represent each social
class for this study (see sec. 1.4.1), a median and mean
social status score was computed for each class (see Table 9).

In this sample the greatest difference in scores appears
between the upper-middle and lower-middle classes. A difference

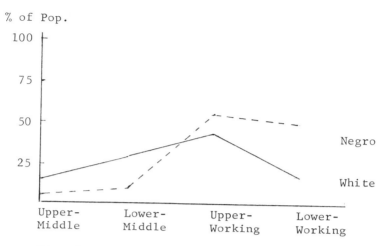

Fig. 5.   Distribution of Negro and White
          Population by Social Class

Table 9

Median and Mean Social Status Scores
for Four Social Classes

Class Designation	Median Social Status Score	Mean Social Status
Upper-middle	32	35.2
Lower-middle	73.5	69.7
Upper-working	97	97.6
Lower-working	119	118.9

of 41.5 points between the medians and 34.5 between the
means is observed. The smallest difference exists between
the upper-working and lower-working classes, where a difference of only 22 points between medians and 21.3 points
between means is revealed. Of the informants chosen for
this study, the greatest social status distance between
classes is indicated between the top two classes and the
smallest distance between the bottom two. An independent

study of class boundaries in the Detroit population by
Landecker (1960) reveals a similar type of pattern.[9] That
is, Landecker notes (1960: 874-875) that, by far, the most
outstanding boundary is found between the group with the
highest social status score and the remainder of the population, and that at the lower end of the social scale it is
very difficult to determine clear-cut boundaries.[10] If
linguistic differences are an accurate reflection of social
stratification, it can be hypothesized that the most clear-
cut linguistic boundaries will parallel the most clear-cut
social boundaries.

It is also possible to show how the social classes compare with one another in relation to the three independent
scales which give the median and mean rank (from 1-7 for
education and occupation, and 1-6 for residency; see Tables
5-8) for each class in terms of the three scales.

Table 10

Median and Mean Score for Education,
Occupation, and Residency Scales

Class	Education Median Mean		Occupation Median Mean		Residency Median Mean	
Upper-middle	1	1.3	1	1.3	3	2.7
Lower-middle	3	3.0	4	3.8	3	3.2
Upper-working	5	4.7	6	5.9	3	3.6
Lower-working	6.5	6.3	6.5	6.4	6	5.3

Table 10 indicates that the educational scale shows a
rather consistent difference between all classes, each class
showing a difference of at least 1.5 with the contiguous
class. Educationally, the upper-middle class is characterized
by college and usually some graduate training, the lower-

middle class by several years of college, the upper-working class by some high school (possibly completed), and the lower-working class by junior high school or less (see Table 4). On the occupation scale, the first three classes show consistent intervals between each class and the next (two or more rankings in each case). The difference between the upper-working and lower- working class is minimal.[11] The residency scale shows the least amount of difference between the upper-middle, lower-middle, and upper-working classes. Between the upper-working and lower-working classes the greatest difference is revealed; in fact, residency seems to be the most singularly important factor in distinguishing the upper-working class from the lower-working class. The minimization of residential differences between the first three classes may be accounted for in part by the housing restrictions on the Negro population in Detroit.[12] The above description of mean and median score for three scales indicates that the different scales do not "naturally" divide the population in the same way. If differences in linguistic behavior correlate with one of the scales (e.g. education) rather than the overall socio-economic rank, it suggests that one of the scales may be more essential than the others in the social stratification of speech.

To sum up, this chapter has set the sociological context which serves as a basis for investigating differences in linguistic behavior. The pattern of racial isolation in Detroit has separated the great majority of the Negro population from the co-existing white population. On the other hand, differences in the relative social status of Negroes have set apart various social classes of Negroes from one another.

NOTES

1. In the census figures there is often no breakdown be-
    tween Negro and other non-white races. A check of those
    figures which do make such a distinction reveals that
    over 99 per cent are Negro. There is little skewing of
    the figures because of the failure to distinguish Negro
    non-white from other non-white in the Detroit Census
    information.

2. If the location within the state were given, one would
    suspect that the Detroit residents who migrated from
    Georgia came from the inland region. An examination of
    the informants used in this study confirms this sus-
    picion.

3. The percentages were obtained by adding the total number
    of whites and Negroes for all census tracts included in
    a given area.

4. The residential area only includes the current residency
    of informants. Previous housing was not taken into con-
    sideration.

5. For the adults, an estimate of integration in schooling
    and present work were combined. For example, a main-
    tenance worker for the city (predominantly Negro), edu-
    cated in the South, would be given a predominantly Negro
    rating. Of necessity, in several instances the rating
    was rather subjective. For the children and teen-agers,
    the percentage of Negroes in schools is based on "Racial
    Distribution of Students and Contract Personnel in the
    Detroit Public Schools" (Board of Education, Detroit,
    Michigan, 1965), which covers the 1965-1966 school year.

6. The model reported in Shuy, Wolfram and Riley (1967) was
    constructed by Dana Downing in consultation with soci-
    ologists from Michigan State University and Wayne State
    University.

7. The different weights were based on previous sociological
    studies which determined the relative significance of
    these factors in estimating overall socio-economic ranking.

8. Although it is assumed in this study that it is feasible
    to delimit discrete social classes (at least for the con-
    venience of presenting statistical tables), students of
    social stratification in the United States disagree about

the actual presence or absence of structural divisions in the American social status system. Some claim that status differences in American society form a continuous gradual hierarchy, whereas others claim that discrete structural hierarchies exist. For a discussion, see Ellis, "Social Stratification and Social Relations: An Empirical Test of the Disjunctiveness of Social Classes" (1957) and Landecker, "Class Boundaries" (1960).

9. Landecker's study is based on both the white and Negro population. This same type of pattern is revealed for only the Negro population.

10. Landecker calls this social group with the highest scores the "elite" group, but his socio-economic profile of this group is equivalent to what is labeled upper-middle class in this classification.

11. Part of the similarity of the upper- and lower-working classes occupationally may be a function of the data collection. Informants who are welfare recipients may give as their present occupation the type of work they did when they were last employed.

12. A cursory examination of 10 randomly selected upper-middle class white informants shows that their residency rank is generally higher than that of the Negroes.

3 THE LINGUISTIC VARIABLES

3.1 The Linguistic Variable

The measurement of sociolinguistic behavior requires the
formulation of a unit which can represent continuous, ordered,
variation within and across discrete linguistic types. The
unit which permits this characterization has been termed the
linguistic variable (Labov 1966b: 15). The linguistic variable, itself an abstraction, is realized in actual speech
behavior by variants; that is, individual items which are
members of a class of variants constituting the variable.
Labov (1966b: 15) notes:

> Whereas the linguistic variant is a particular item --
> a morph or a phone -- the variable is a class of variants
> which are ordered along a continuous dimension and whose
> position is determined by an independent linguistic or
> extra-linguistic variable.

The variants of a given linguistic variable may be part
of one or more structural units (e.g. phoneme or morpheme)
within a linguistic system. Traditionally, the linguistic
variable has been used with reference to variants within one
linguistic system, but it is also possible to extend the
concept of the linguistic variable to include variants which
may be members of distinct but co-existing language codes.
As will be seen in this analysis, it is possible for a given
linguistic variable to include some variants which may be
defined as part of the NNE system and others which are part
of the SE system.

The formulation of the linguistic variable has dividends
for linguistics in general and sociolinguistics in particular
because it is the unit which serves as a basis for correlating
linguistic variation with extra-linguistic or independent
linguistic factors. The particular value of a given linguistic variable (x) may be viewed as a function (f) of its correlation with extra-linguistic or independent linguistic
variables. For example, in this analysis, the value of each
linguistic variable is viewed as a function of its correlation with socio-economic class, racial isolation, age, sex,
and contextual style. This is represented formulaically as:

$$x = f\ (a,\ b,\ c,\ d,\ e)$$

where a = socio-economic class

b = racial isolation

c = age

d = sex

e = contextual style

The regularity with which much variation, formerly dismissed as "free variation", can be accounted for on the basis
of extra-linguistic factors has made the concept of the
linguistic variable an invaluable construct in the description of patterned speech variation.[1]

3.2 The Relation of Variants to NNE and SE Systems

The variables we are dealing with may have variants which are
members of distinct but overlapping language varieties. This
fact forces us to ask what relationships these variants have
to one another in terms of the two systems. One can, of
course, dismiss this issue by assuming that all instances of
variation between SE and NNE features are simply matters of
"code-switching".[2] From this perspective, if a SE variant
is observed in a person's speech where NNE features are predominant, it is assumed to be an instance of code-switching.

This assumption weakens the notion of code-switching beyond
usefulness. In the first place, code-switching involves a
SET (i.e. a set of grammatical and phonological variants)
rather than isolated variants. A bilingual speaker switching
codes has a distinct set of grammatical and phonological
variables associated with the switch. Sporadic occurrences of
features which are part of another system are viewed as borrowing or interference from that system (Weinreich 1953: 7).
In the second place, switching usually takes place in response
to some stylistic, situational, interlocutor, topic, or some
other functional shift. It is doubtful that relatively isolated instances of features associated with a fairly constant
contextual style can be considered instances of code-switching
(see Weinreich 1953: 73-74). A more reasonable suggestion is
that there is interference or dialect mixture from co-existent
codes.[3] This does not mean that instances of code-switching
do not occur. They do occur as a SET of linguistic features
is changed in response to a functional shift. But in the
analysis of a relatively constant contextual situation, the
role of interference and dialect mixture takes precedence
over code-switching in describing the empirical data.[4]

If we assume that we are not simply dealing with code-
switching we are faced with the question, what is the distinction between "dialect mixture" (i.e. variant forms which
are importations from another dialect) and what Labov (1968)
has called "inherent variability" (i.e. variant forms which
are an integral part of the vernacular)?[5] The distinction
between dialect mixture and inherent variability is especially
important for the investigator of a nonstandard language
variety which has had considerable contact with a more prestigious standard variety. One may dismiss the notion of
inherent variability by assuming that any obligatory rule in
SE which has to be designated as optional in describing the

speech behavior of NNE speakers be considered an importation from SE. For example, the presence of the copula in SE is obligatory in certain environments (he's nice). In these same environments it is sometimes absent and other times present in speakers of NNE. If one does not admit inherent variability, its presence has to be interpreted as an importation from SE. One problem with this assumption is that unwanted variants may automatically be set aside as examples of dialect mixture, with only those forms most different from SE being reported.

On the other hand, one can dismiss the notion of dialect mixture by assuming that any feature occurring among NNE speakers be described as an integral part of the NNE system. For example, -Z, third person singular present tense morpheme, categorically present with most verbs in SE, occurs only infrequently among some NNE speakers. The relative infrequency of this form is viewed as irrelevant in describing the NNE system, as long as it does occur at one time or another. The problem with this position is that it denies the fundamental dynamics of language contact, in which a form is borrowed without its systematic integration into a recipient language or dialect.

The alternative to the above categorical assumptions is to admit both inherent variability and dialect mixture. Although this alternative presents a somewhat unwieldy problem in distinguishing between the two, it is consistent with the actual facts of language structure and language contact situations. Quantitative evidence combined with structural clues of basic unfamiliarity with the rules which govern the form in question is the essential factor in designating certain forms occurring among NNE speakers as importations from SE. The most important type of quantitative evidence for dialect mixture is the patterned decrease in the frequency of a form

the further one gets from a contextual situation socially
advantageous for the use of SE. If feature x, obligatory
in a given environment in SE, occurs 30 per cent of the time
in that environment in a speech situation most advantageous
for the use of SE (e.g. school) and only 5 per cent in a
casual speech situation (e.g. peer group interaction), one
infers from the frequency patterning that the item is an
importation from SE and not present in an ideal grammatical
construct of NNE.

Structural clues are also important in designating forms
as importations from SE. As an example, we may anticipate
our discussion of suffixal -Z, which occurs with third person
singular present tense verb forms (see sec. 5.1.1). In SE,
-Z combines categorically with most third person singular
present tense verbs (e.g. he goes), but never occurs with
non-third person forms. Among speakers of NNE, it is observed that -Z does not categorically occur with third person
singular forms. Furthermore, it is sometimes found on non-
third person singular forms (e.g. I goes). Occasionally, it
is even found on infinite or other non-finite verb forms
(e.g. to goes). The non-categorical occurrence of -Z with
third person singular present tense forms, combined with its
occasional occurrence on non-third person singular and non-
finite forms, suggests that NNE speakers have a basic unfamiliarity with the SE rules governing -Z occurrence. Its
occurrence with non-third person singular forms may be a
type of hypercorrection by NNE speakers who realize that -Z
occurs with verb forms, but are unfamiliar with its co-
occurrence restrictions.

Quantitative and structural evidence serve as a basis
for designating the occurrence of certain forms as SE importations in this analysis. If there is no quantitative or
structural evidence indicating that a given form is an

importation, fluctuation between it and another form are considered as inherent variability.[6]

3.3 The Use of Quantitative Methods

The study of linguistic variables rather than categorical
constants adds a new dimension to the examination of speech
differences, namely, the quantitative measurement of the
fluctuation between the variants of a variable. As quantitative methods are utilized, correlations between linguistic
and social patterns emerge. The utilization of quantitative
methods is somewhat of a paradox in linguistics, since structural linguistics has been based traditionally on the analysis
of various continuous dimensions into discrete qualitative
units, conceived as absolutely different from one another.
That a qualitative model is adequate for the description of
a language when viewed as CODE (i.e. its cognitive function)
can hardly be disputed. However, the functions of language
when viewed as BEHAVIOR (i.e. its social function) suggest
that a qualitative model is inadequate in accounting for the
patterned variation between forms.

The quantitative measurement of linguistic variables
necessarily involves counting variants. Measuring the frequency of variants may, at first, seem to be a fairly simple
procedure. But Labov (1968: 14) has correctly pointed out:

> ...even the simplest type of counting raises a number
> of subtle and difficult problems. The final decision
> as to what to count is actually the final solution to
> the problem at hand. This decision is approached only
> through a long series of exploratory maneuvers.

In the first place, it is necessary to delimit the number of variants which can reliably be identified and to
select relevant categories of variants for tabulation. For
example, it will be seen in the tabulation of syllable-final
d (see sec. 4.3) that only three categories of variants are

relevant for tabulation, although at least six different
phonetic variants may be identified.

It is also important to identify the total population
of utterances in which an item may "potentially" vary (Labov
1968: 14). For example, in the discussion of the copula
(see sec. 5.3) there are certain types of syntactic constructions in which the presence of the copula is obligatory for
ALL speakers; in other types of syntactic constructions the
copula may or may not be present. To include both types of
constructions in a quantitative measurement of variation is
to skew the actual figures of variation.

Further, it is necessary to identify relevant linguistic
environments (phonological, grammatical, and semological)
which may affect the variation of items. In identifying and
classifying different types of environments affecting variation, it is also necessary to exclude environments in which
distinctions between variants are neutralized for phonetic
reasons. Thus, in word-final consonant clusters it is necessary to exclude clusters which are immediately followed by a
homorganic stop (e.g. test day) from the tabulation since it
is sometimes impossible to determine whether the final consonant of the cluster is present or absent. The importance
of identifying relevant linguistic environments for quantitative measurement cannot be overestimated.

Specifically turning to the selection of linguistic variables for quantitative sociolinguistic study, Labov (1964a:
166) has suggested that several criteria are essential in
selecting a linguistic variable. These may be enumerated as
follows:

(1) The variable should be high in frequency.

(2) The variable should have a certain immunity from con-
     scious suppression.

(3) The variable should be an integral part of a larger
     structure.

(4) The variable should be easily quantifiable on a linear
     scale.

According to Labov (1964a: 176), syntactical and morphological variables are less useful for quantitative measurement because of their low frequency and their susceptability
to conscious suppression. The problem of low frequency can
be somewhat neutralized by selecting texts sufficient in
length to guarantee that certain types of grammatical features
will occur with some degree of regularity. Although some
grammatical features may tend to be more consciously sup-
pressed than phonological features, this is a valid reason
for excluding grammatical features from quantitative study
only if there is TOTAL suppression by practically the whole
sample population (e.g. as certain taboo words in a tape-
recorded interview). The fact that certain social groups
show a qualitative absence of a socially "stigmatized" grammatical feature in an interview situation, rather than a
disadvantage, is considered an important factor in observing
the relations between phonological and grammatical variables
as they correlate with social differences.

3.4 The Variables

Having discussed the concept of the linguistic variable as
it applies to sociolinguistic research, we may now identify
the phonological and grammatical variables which will be
examined in this study. Although phonological and grammatical
variables are discussed separately, it must be noted that
several of the variables show considerable intersection between grammar and phonology.

3.4.1 The Phonological Variables

(1) Word-Final Consonant Clusters

The absence of the second member of word-final consonant
clusters has been cited (Labov, Cohen and Robins 1965: 35)

as one of the most important variables in the sound patterns
of Negro speakers.[7] This variable may affect uninflected
lexical forms ending in clusters (referred to by Labov, et
al. [1965: 36] as <u>monomorphemic</u> clusters, since the whole
cluster occurs in only one morphemic unit). It also intersects with the grammatical system by operating on forms where
the final member of the cluster, orthographically represented
by the suffix -<u>ed</u>, is a grammatical signal (referred to in
this study as <u>bimorphemic</u> clusters since each member of the
cluster occurs in a different morphemic unit). This variable includes a number of different word-final cluster combinations which may be summarized in Table 11.

Table 11

Consonant Clusters in which the Final Member
of the Cluster may be Absent

Cluster	Examples[8]	
	Monomorphemic	Bimorphemic
[st]	test, post, list	missed, messed, dressed
[sp]	wasp, clasp, grasp	
[sk]	desk, risk, mask	
[št]		finished, latched, cashed
[zd]		raised, composed, amazed
[žd][9]		judged, charged, forged
[ft]	left, craft, cleft	laughed, stuffed, roughed
[vd]		loved, lived, moved
[nd]	mind, find, mound	rained, fanned, canned
[md]		named, foamed, rammed
[ld]	cold, wild, old	called, smelled, killed
[pt]	apt, adept, inept	mapped, stopped, clapped
[kt]	act, contact, expect	looked, cooked, cracked

In Table 11, it is observed that both members of the
cluster are either voiced or voiceless. Clusters in which

voicing or voicelessness is not a defining characteristic of
the entire cluster such as [mp] (e.g. jump), [nt] (e.g. count),
[lt] (e.g. colt), [ŋk] (e.g. crank), and [lp] (e.g. gulp) are
not included in this analysis since they do not function in
the same way as the above list.

(2) Morpheme Medial and Final θ

One of the most frequently observed phonological differences between the speech of some Negroes and white speakers
of a Midwestern variety of SE is the correspondence of a
voiceless labiodental fricative [f] with a voiceless interdental fricative [θ].[10] This correspondence typically can
be found in such words as tooth, with, athletic, nothing,
and Catholic. The correspondence is actually part of a more
regular pattern in which both voiceless and voiced inter-
dentals, [θ] and [ð] (both of which are represented orthographically as th), correspond to labiodental fricatives [f]
and [v], respectively. Although [f] is the most predominant
correspondence to SE [θ], several other variants occurring
in particular environments and/or with particular lexical
items must be noted. These include [t] and [∅] (i.e. no
phonetic realization at all) in words such as nothing and
with.

(3) Syllable-Final d

In syllable-final position, voiced stops b, d, and g
(and to a lesser extent, all voiced obstruent consonants)
reveal variants not generally described for SE. The voiced
alveolar stop d, the most frequently occurring member of this
set, is chosen for description. The significant categories
of variants are a glottal stop [ʔ] or unreleased voiceless
alveolar stop [t˺] and the complete absence of a consonant.
Typical words which are meaningful for examining the distribution of these variants are good, bed, bad, and shed. Although this feature has been less frequently recognized than

other phonological features, it is useful in describing the
speech behavior of the Negro community in its social context.

(4)   Post-Vocalic r

The absence of post-vocalic r in such words as sister,
beard, fair, Saturday, fire has been shown to have both
regional and social distribution in certain areas of the
United States (see Kurath 1941, McDavid 1948, Labov 1966a).
In certain Northern urban areas in which the regional pattern for white speakers includes the consistent phonetic
realization of post-vocalic -r, the absence of this feature
has taken on specialized social significance for the Negro
population. The basic contrast is between the presence and
absence of some type of constriction. Although "r-lessness"
occurs in other than post-vocalic position among some members
of the Negro population (e.g. [bəvə] 'brother'), the data are
restricted to an analysis of r in post-vocalic position.

3.4.2   The Grammatical Variables

(1)   Zero Copula

A well-known characteristic of some Negro speakers is
the absence of the copula be in a variety of syntactical
environments. These environments include: (1) predicate
nominal (Dolores the vice-president. 444:12);[11] (2) predicate
adjective (She nice. 583:13); (3) predicate locative (He at
Northwestern. 583:11); (4) verb -ing (We going Friday night.
447:15); and (5) intentional future gonna (It's something you
gonna have. 565:27). Although this variable is categorized
here as grammatical, Labov (1968) has suggested that the
absence of copula is due to a phonological process operating
on contracted forms. Prior to Labov's study, the absence of
copula had been considered primarily a grammatical feature.

(2)   Invariant Be

Another NNE form which has received considerable attention

recently is the use of the form be as a finite verb (e.g. The problems always be wrong. 521:15). Recent interpretations of this form by Loflin (forthcoming), Feigenbaum (forthcoming), Fasold (forthcoming), and Labov, et al. (1968) differ somewhat, but all emphasize that a unique sememic unit underlies the use of this form in NNE.

On the basis of adverb co-occurrence restrictions, in some environments the form has an iterative or habitual meaning which is unique to NNE speakers (Sometime she be fighting in school. 444:29; He usually be up. 565:55). Fasold (forthcoming) and Labov, et al. (1968) have noted that in other environments the use of this form appears to function as a type of future with an underlying (i.e. on a different stratum in the language code) will or would in its structure (e.g. He be in in a few minutes. 447:4; I be twelve February seven. 461:41).

Although this variable is treated primarily as grammatical, its use as a type of future (with a zero realization of will or would) suggests that there may be an intersection of phonology with grammar.

(3) Suffixal -Z

In SE the morphemic suffix represented by -Z (with it morphophonemically defined alternants -ɪz, -z, and -s) is the realization of several lexemic units including:[12]
(1) third person singular present morpheme (e.g. he talks);
(2) possessive marker (e.g. John's book); and (3) plural marker (e.g. three years).[13] All of these lexemic units which are realized by -Z have been observed to be absent in at least certain types of environments as can be seen in the following examples:

Third Person Singular Present Tense

He stand on his hind legs. 304:4

Sometime she write on both of them. 489:21

Possessive

He was really my grandfather dog. 489:17

Sometimes we play with my brother and friends, my
brother friends. 370:4

Plural

I wish I had a million dollar. 370:4

She stayed down there and farmed with me for two
year. 506:35

In the actual treatment of this variable, it is divided
into three sub-categories and the relation between these subcategories is examined.

(4) Multiple Negation

One of the well-known grammatical features distinguishing different social groups in the United States is the so-
called "double negative" (but referred to here as multiple
negation, since it is a more accurate statement of the formulation of this particular type of negative concord). Multiple
negation may occur when a negative sentence occurs with:
(1) an indefinite adverb (e.g. I couldn't hardly pick him up.
278:21); (2) an indefinite pronoun (e.g. I don't bother
nobody. 447:20); or (3) indefinite determiner (e.g. They
didn't have no gym. 506:6). Although multiple negation is
a feature of both white and Negro nonstandard speech, there
are several patterns of multiple negation which are distinct
to Negro speakers (see sec. 5.2 for a discussion of the differences between white and Negro nonstandard in relation to
this feature). Where multiple negation might occur (i.e. a
negative sentence in which an indefinite adverb, pronoun, or
determiner occurs) one may divide the utterances into "realized" and "unrealized" multiple negatives.

NOTES

1. The fact that much linguistic variation can be accounted
   for by introducing extra-linguistic factors does NOT, as
   some have interpreted, completely obliterate the notion
   of free variation. Labov notes:

   > Free variation certainly exists, in the sense of
   > irreducible fluctuations in the sounds of a language
   > without any one significant conditioning factor.
   > The characteristic step in the misapplication of
   > "free variation" in linguistics is to assume the
   > absence of significant causes or conditions without
   > empirical investigation (1966b: 5).

2. "Code-switching" is defined here as a shift from one
   linguistic system to another by a speaker who has acquired two or more systems.

3. Interference is used to refer to the process in which a
   speaker is unable to adopt the norms of a target language or dialect because of the imposition of constraints
   from a source language or dialect. Dialect mixture refers to the result of merging features from more than one
   language variety.

4. Another factor in asserting the place of interference or
   dialect mixture as opposed to code-switching is the considerable overlap between the systems. The closer the
   two systems are, the more important the matter of interference or dialect mixture becomes.

5. Inherent variability, from a categorical view of language,
   is synonymous with free variation within one variety of
   a language code.

6. The designating of fluctuation between forms as inherent
   variability does not mean that historically both forms
   were necessarily an integral part of the system. Inherent
   variability is only considered from a synchronic viewpoint.

7. The term absence is deliberately used to avoid commitment
   to a process formulation implicit in the terms reduction
   or simplification, which are often associated with the
   discussion of this phenomenon.

8. Where examples are absent under either the monomorphemic
    or bimorphemic category, the cluster is not found under
    the particular category.

9. The cluster [žd] only occurs in the affricated form
    (i.e. [džd]) in word-final position, whereas the cluster
    [št] occurs in both an affricated and non-affricated form.

10. The term substitution has sometimes been used where the
    term correspondence is used in this study. Correspondence,
    the linguistically appropriate term for the type of re-
    lation observed between the sounds, does not have the
    normative connotations that the term substitution seems
    to have.

11. The tape number of the informant and page or "bit" number
    on which the example is found in the transcript are indi-
    cated immediately following examples taken from my corpus.

12. The terms lexemic and morphemic are used in the sense
    employed by Lamb (1966b: 29-31). They represent two
    substrata within the grammatical stratum of the language
    code.

13. On a select subset of adverbs (e.g. sometimes, besides)
    it is also possible to interpret -Z as a type of ad-
    verbial marker.

4 PHONOLOGICAL VARIABLES

Having presented in the preceding chapters the sociological
and linguistic background necessary to discuss the linguistic
correlates of social stratification, we now turn to the
actual discussion of the social significance of linguistic
variables. In this chapter the phonological variables delimited in Section 3.4.2 will be discussed, first independently, then as they relate to a unified view of their social
significance.

4.1 Word-Final Consonant Clusters

4.1.1 General Procedures

The two basic categories relevant in viewing the social significance of the consonant clusters listed in Table 11 (see
p. 50) are simply the absence and the presence of the stop
which is the final member of the cluster. There are variants
of the first member of the cluster which may have social
significance in themselves but are not considered as a separate category here. For example, nasal + stop clusters may
be realized simply as vowel nasalization (e.g. [frɛ̃ə]
'friend'); likewise, lateral + stop clusters may be realized
by vocalization or complete absence of both a lateral and
stop (e.g. [toʊ] 'told'). Although variants of the first
member of the cluster were consistently observed for some
types of clusters, only the presence or absence of the final
stop is considered significant in the quantitative measurement
of the variable.

In measuring this variable, the following procedures for
tabulation were adopted:

(1)   Beginning with Section I B of the interview (see Appen-
      dix B), dealing with the narration of a TV program or
      movie, the first 20 instances in which a monomorphemic
      cluster might occur were tabulated for each informant.

(2)   Beginning with Section I B, the first 15 examples of
      bimorphemic clusters were tabulated for each informant.

(3)   If the same word occurred more than three times, only
      the first three examples were taken in order not to
      skew the data with too many tokens for one particular
      type.

(4)   Clusters which were immediately followed by a homorganic
      stop (e.g. test day) were excluded from the tabulation
      since it was impossible to perceive from the tape re-
      cordings whether the final stop was absent or present
      because of the phonetic environment.

The first two procedures were adopted in order to maintain uniformity in the contextual style and the number of
items which was counted for each informant. The contextual style
which is used as the basis of measurement in this investigation combines two of Labov's five contextual styles, namely,
what he calls "careful" and "casual" speech. According to
Labov (1966a: 100-111), casual speech in an interview situation is defined by specialized contexts (e.g. discussion not
in direct answer to a question, speech directed to a third
person, etc.) and paralinguistic "channel cues" such as changes
in tempo, pitch, laughter, or heavy breathing. An exploratory
attempt to distinguish careful from casual speech based on
Labov's criteria was rejected for several reasons. In the
first place, any of the paralinguistic channel cues cited as
indications of casual speech can also be indications that the
informant feels an increased awareness of the artificiality
or formality of the interview situation. Can nervous laughter
reliably be distinguished from relaxed or casual laughter?

Also, the subjective interpretation of the paralinguistic cues tends to bias the interpretation of casual speech even though the channel cues are theoretically supposed to be independent of the measurement of linguistic variables. To what extent must there be a change of pitch or rhythm and how close to the actual feature being tabulated must it occur? Further, for some informants, the incidence of casual speech, based on Labov's cues, is so infrequent that it is difficult to base statistics on so few examples. Thus, narrative passages as comparable as possible within an interview situation were used and no attempt was made to distinguish careful from casual speech using Labov's criteria.

Bimorphemic and monomorphemic clusters were tabulated separately. This was done in order to examine the different types of clusters without assuming that the same type of phonological pattern prevails for both of them. In order to examine the possibility that the absence of -ed verbal suffix actually results from a grammatical rather than a phonological pattern (see Loflin 1967b: 14-16, for a grammatical interpretation of the absence of bimorphemic clusters) bimorphemic clusters were tabulated separately. Bimorphemic clusters include -ed when associated with past tense (e.g. Yesterday he moved away), passive (e.g. The boy was messed up) or noun modification[1] (pre-noun, e.g. the scratched arm, or embedded noun phrases, e.g. the dude named Alfred) although its association with the past tense is by far the most frequent. Only those contexts where past time was clearly unambiguous were tabulated (e.g. He was messed up; Yesterday he messed up).

4.1.2 The Correlation of Monomorphemic Clusters with Social Class

In Fig. 6 the percentage of clusters in which the final stop

is absent is given for the upper-middle class white group
(abbreviated henceforth as UMW) used as the SE sample, and
the four social classes of Negroes, upper-middle, lower-
middle, upper-working, and lower-working class (abbreviated
as UMN, LMN, UWN, and LWN, respectively). In the accompanying tabulation both the mean and median percentages for each
social group are given.

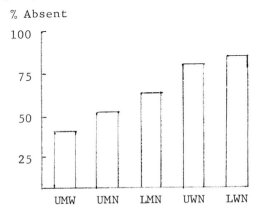

Percentage of Final Cluster
Member Absent

	Mean	Median
UMW	38.7	40.0
UMN	51.0	54.0
LMN	65.9	62.5
UWN	79.2	80.0
LWN	84.2	82.5

Fig. 6.   Absence of Final Cluster Member
in Monomorphemic Clusters: By
Social Class

According to Fig. 6, the absence of the final cluster
member is found on all social levels, the classes being
distinguished by quantitative differences. The UMN group
and the SE white group of the same level clearly indicate a
difference in the percentage of cluster-final stops which

are absent even though the difference is less between the
median than the mean scores. The fact that the median scores
are closer than the mean scores for these two groups indicates that the frequency distribution of final stop absence
shows more fluctuation between the individual UMN informants
than the UMW informants.

Fig. 6 does not distinguish the possible effect of phonetic environment on the absence of the final stop in the
consonant cluster. Labov and Cohen (1967: 69), however, have
called attention to the importance of consonantal and vocalic
environments following the potential cluster. Actually, the
crucial distinction is between environments in which a consonant follows immediately and those in which it does not.
Thus, we may distinguish between non-consonantal, which includes a vowel (whether it be part of a lexical item beginning with a vowel or a vocalic hesitation segment), pause,
or terminal juncture, and a consonantal environment. In
Fig. 7 the incidence of final stop absence for monomorphemic
clusters is given for these two environments. The percentages are based on the combined figures for all informants in
the social group rather than giving mean or median scores.[2]

The effect of the non-consonantal environment in reducing the frequency of final stop absence shows the importance of distinguishing the two environments. It is also
observed that the discrepancy between the social groups is
much greater when followed by a non-consonantal environment
than when followed by a consonant. The sharp demarcation of
the classes in the non-consonantal environment suggests that
this environment is considerably more "socially diagnostic"
than the consonantal environment. That is, the difference
between social classes is much more obvious in the non-
consonantal environment.

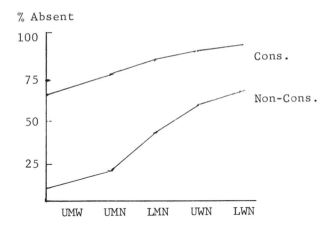

% Absent

Percentage of Final Cluster
Member Absent when Followed
by Consonantal and Non-
Consonantal Environments

	Cons.	Non-Cons.
UMW	66.4	11.5
UMN	78.9	22.6
LMN	86.7	43.3
UWN	93.5	65.4
LWN	97.3	72.1

Fig. 7. Effect of Following Environment on
Absence of Final Member of Monomorphemic Cluster: By Social Class

One may analyze the environments further, as to the type
of consonant or non-consonantal environment which precedes or
follows the potential cluster. An attempt to define different types of following consonantal environments for UMW and
UMN informants indicates that the type of consonant does have
some effect on the absence of the final stop. When the following consonant is the same as the first member of the consonant cluster (test score), the final consonant is absent
87.5 per cent of the time. When it is followed by resonant

consonants such as w, y, h, or r, it is absent only 42.4 per
cent.

The low frequency with which the final cluster member is
absent when followed by a non-consonantal environment among
UMW informants (11.5) causes one to suspect that, in SE, the
presence of the final cluster member in this environment is
obligatory. Most instances of absence for this group are
restricted to polysyllabic words (e.g. breakfast, playground)
and a select subset of lexical items, the chief member of
which is unstressed just [jɪs]). When these words are eliminated from the tabulation for the UMW, the percentages are
lowered considerably (to 3.3 per cent absence). With these
restrictions in mind, one may suggest that before a non-
consonantal environment the presence of the cluster-final
stop, for all practical purposes, is categorically present
in SE. The underlying form (i.e. the morphophoneme) is the
full cluster, the final member simply being realized as zero
in certain environments. The matter is less clear-cut for
the working-class Negro populations, where the absence of
the final cluster member does not approach categorical presence in this environment. One then can ask if the same
underlying form exists among NNE speakers.

An important consideration in viewing the underlying
form of NNE speakers is the effect that a suffix has on a
potential cluster. It is essential to observe what happens
when -s plural is added to words whose stems potentially
end in st.

The morphophonemic alternants of the -s plural (in
both SE and NNE) are quite regular: -ɪz following forms ending in sibilants (e.g. /rowzɪz/ 'roses'), -s following other
voiceless segments (e.g. /kæts/ 'cats'), and -z following
other voiced segments (e.g. /bədz/ 'buds'). Because the -s
plural has different morphophonemic alternates depending

on whether a stem ends in sibilant or stop, we ask if, for
NNE speakers, the plural form operates as if the final stop
is present or whether it operates as if the final segment is
a sibilant. Table 12 presents the plural formation for items
potentially ending in a sibilant + stop cluster when pluralized.[3] Four different types of pluralization were noted and
transcribed:

(1)   The complete cluster (with either t or k as the stop)
      plus -s plural (e.g. [dɛsks] or [dɛsts]).

(2)   The realization of a stop, but compensatory lengthening
      of the sibilant which occurs as a part of the cluster
      instead of a -s plural attached to the cluster (e.g.
      [dɛs:k]).

(3)   The absence of a stop but compensatory lengthening of
      the sibilant (e.g. [dɛs:]).

(4)   The absence of a stop and addition of -ɨz plural (e.g.
      [dɛsɨz]).

Table 12
Distribution of Informants by Pluralization
of Sibilant + Stop Cluster: By Social Class

	[dɛsks] No. of Inf.	[dɛs:k] No. of Inf.	[dɛs:] No. of Inf.	[dɛsɨz] No. of Inf.
UMW	5	2	3	-
UMN	4	5	2	-
LMN	3	4	4	-
UWN	-	-	4	5
LWN	-	-	1	7

The social distribution of pluralization indicated in
Table 12 is significant. Although the SE white group and
middle-class Negro groups fluctuate between the first three
categories, the formation of the -ɨz plural is completely
restricted to the working-class group.

The fact that morphophonemic alternants of the plural

operate as if the form ended in a sibilant suggests that the
correspondence of SE word-final clusters in NNE is simply
the first member of the cluster (i.e. SE [dɛsk] = NNE [dɛs]).

Before concluding that the underlying form for NNE
speakers is a simple consonant, the form which occurs when
other types of suffixes beginning with a vowel are added,
including comparative -er, superlative -est, participial
-ing, and past or participial -ed must be noted. Although
the incidence of this type of combination is too infrequent
for quantitative measurement, the examples in the corpus
indicate that in these combinations both members of the
cluster are regularly realized (e.g. [fæstɨs] 'fastest',
[rɛstɨn] 'resting', [bəstɨd] 'busted').[4] The -ed suffix
following a cluster-final alveolar stop (e.g. interested,
busted) is the most significant of these suffixes because
of its morphophonemic alternation: -ɨd following alveolar
stops, t following voiceless stops, and d following voiced
stops. If the underlying form did not end in an alveolar
stop, /t/ or /d/ would be the predominant realization of the
-ed suffix. Yet, in 13 out of 15 cases found for UWN and
LWN informants, /-ɨd/ was the realized form. The fact that
when a suffix beginning with a vowel is added, both members of
the cluster are present suggests that the underlying form includes both members, the final members being realized as
zero only when word final. On the other hand, the evidence
of the plural suffix in Table 12 indicates that the morphophonemic alternation operates on the sibilant and not on the
stop. One must ask if the formation of the -s plural is
not a specialized adaptation (ordered in the sense that it
operates on the zero realization of the cluster-final stop)
of NNE speakers to the phonetic sequence s + stop + s. Both
NNE and SE speakers have compensatory ways of realizing this
sequence without having to articulate the s + stop + s sequence.

Among the working-class speakers a different adaptation is
maintained, in keeping with the pattern of realizing st as
s in a number of environments.

One explanation for the regular presence of both members
with most suffixes beginning with a vowel is the possibility
of reassigning syllable boundaries so that the stop is now
reassigned as the first member of the following syllable,
e.g. fas + ter (see Labov, et al. 1968: 123). NNE does not
favor syllables ending in clusters. This syllable reassign-
ment does not consistently operate across word boundaries,

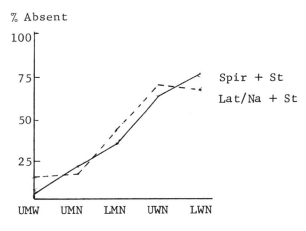

% Absent

Spir + St

Lat/Na + St

UMW   UMN   LMN   UWN   LWN

Percentage of Final Cluster
Member Absent in Spirant +
Stop and Lateral/Nasal +
Stop Clusters

	Spirant+St	Lat/Na+St
UMW	6.9	12.7
UMN	22.0	19.7
LMN	36.8	42.9
UWN	63.9	71.6
LWN	75.5	68.6

Fig. 8.   Comparison of Spirant + Stop and Lateral/
          Nasal + Stop Monomorphemic Clusters when
          Followed by a Non-consonantal Environment:
          By Social Class

so that in word-final position the cluster-final stop is NOT
necessarily reassigned as the first member of the following
syllable when the following word begins with a vowel (e.g.
/fæs # ælfrɪd/ but not /fæs # tælfrɪd/ 'fast Alfred').

Finally, one can also examine the clusters on the basis
of the type of consonant which potentially combines with the
final stop. A three-way breakdown, based on manner of articulation, is appropriate: (1) lateral or nasal + stop; (2) spirant + stop; and (3) stop + stop clusters. Sufficient quan-
tities for tabulation are only found in the first two categories. These are presented in Fig. 8.

There is no drastic difference in the pattern of zero
realization for the two types of consonant clusters, although
the final member of a sibilant + stop cluster is somewhat
higher than the lateral/nasal + stop clusters for the LWN
class.[5] The same general pattern of final stop absence is
observed for several different types of clusters.

4.1.3   The Correlation of Bimorphemic Clusters
with Social Class

In Fig. 9 the social distribution of the absence of cluster-
final stops is indicated for bimorphemic clusters. Consonant
and non-consonantal environments are distinguished as they
were for monomorphemic clusters.

Several observations can be made on the basis of Fig. 9.
In the first place, as in the monomorphemic clusters, the
non-consonantal environment sharply increases the presence
of the final member of the cluster for all social groups.
An important consideration, not indicated in the percentage
scores given in Fig. 9, is the fact that for most of the UMW
and UMN informants there is a categorical presence of the
final stop when followed by a non-consonantal environment.
Ten out of twelve UMW and seven out of twelve UMN informants
reveal the categorical presence of the final stop in the

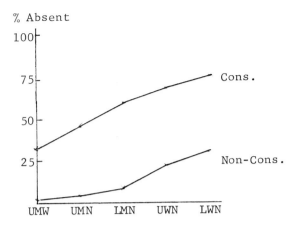

Percentage of Final Cluster
Member Absent when Followed
by Consonantal and Non-
Consonantal Environments

	Cons.	Non-Cons.
UMW	36.2	2.8
UMN	49.2	6.8
LMN	61.7	13.3
UWN	72.5	24.3
LWN	76.0	33.9

Fig. 9.   Absence of Final Cluster Member in Bimor-
          phemic Clusters when Followed by a Conson-
          antal or Non-Consonantal Environment:
          By Social Class

non-consonantal environment. Thus, for most UMW and UMN informants, there is a qualitative difference between them and
informants in the other social groups.

In Fig. 10 the monomorphemic and bimorphemic clusters
are compared in consonantal and non-consonantal environments
(for percentage scores, see Figs. 7 and 9).

From Fig. 10 it appears that the patterning for monomorphemic and bimorphemic clusters operates in much the same
way. Except for the lower frequency of absence in bimorphemic

clusters for all social classes, the type of pattern and
effect of phonetic environment are the same. The fact that
bimorphemic clusters involve a final segment which is a
grammatical signal can be cited to account for the consistently lower frequency of absence. The more information contained in a segment, the less likely it is to be absent.

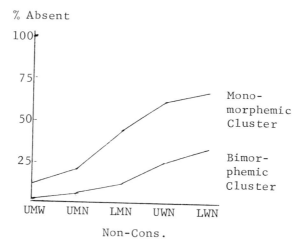

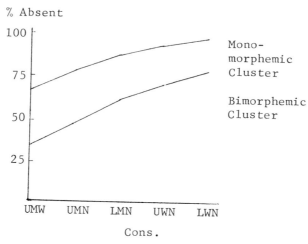

Fig. 10. Comparison of Monomorphemic and Bimor-
          phemic Clusters when Followed by a Non-
          Consonantal and a Consonantal Environment:
          By Social Class

Bimorphemic clusters can be divided into types of consonant clusters on the basis of manner of articulation as
was done for the monomorphemic clusters. Fig. 11 presents
the relative frequency of cluster-final stop absence according to: (1) lateral/nasal + stop; (2) stop + stop; and (3)
spirant + stop. The tabulation only includes clusters when
followed by a non-consonantal environment.

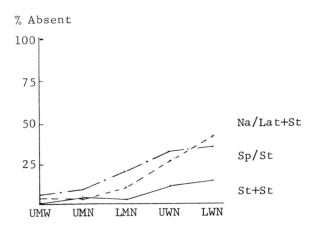

Percentage of Final Cluster
Member Absent

	St+St	NA/Lat+St	Sp+St
UMW	0.0	3.0	3.8
UMN	4.0	3.6	11.9
LMN	3.3	14.7	20.6
UWN	12.1	25.0	31.5
LWN	16.1	40.7	34.3

Fig. 11. Comparison of Stop + Stop, Nasal/Lateral +
          Stop, and Spirant + Stop Bimorphemic Clusters
          when Followed by a Non-Consonantal Environ-
          ment: By Social Class

The percentages for final stop absence are considerably
closer between spirant + stop and nasal/lateral + stop clusters
than they are between stop + stop and the other two types of

clusters. Particularly for the working-class informants,
where final stop absence is a fairly regular pattern, the
stop + stop clusters show a lower percentage of absence than
the spirant + stop and nasal/lateral + stop. In spirant +
stop and nasal/lateral + stop clusters, the first member of
the cluster is a continuant (i.e. a sound during which there
is no complete stoppage of the air stream). If the scores
for continuant + stop clusters are contrasted with those for
stop + stop clusters (see Fig. 12), the difference between
the two types of clusters is significant. How can one possibly account for this difference in the relative frequency
of the two types of clusters based on the different phonetic
compositions? With continuant + stop clusters, the continuant is often lengthened when the final stop is absent (e.g.
[mɛs:əp] 'messed up'). This lengthening can compensate for
the absence of the final stop. With voiceless stop consonants, the same type of lengthening does not generally occur.
Thus, the observed difference in frequency lies in the potential for lengthening that is found in the continuants as
opposed to stops. Until further quantitative study, and more
reliable transcription of length can be achieved, this interpretation is only tentatively proposed as an explanation for
the frequency differences between the various types of clusters.

   At this point, the possibility that the absence of final
cluster members results from a grammatical rather than a
phonological difference in the uses of -ed past tense in SE
and NNE must be analyzed. It cannot be denied that some
differences in tense concord may exist between the two systems.
One may ask if what has been counted is actually grammatical
differences and not phonological patterning at all. Loflin
(1967b: 11-16), maintains that the lack of cluster-final stops
is grammatical:

...I have opted in the direction of a grammatical
solution to explain the absence of -ed because,
on the one hand, a grammatical category (Genr) is
already needed to account for the set of zero
marked verbs...and, on the other hand, no consistent
pattern of phonological or morphological conditioning
has yet been determined.

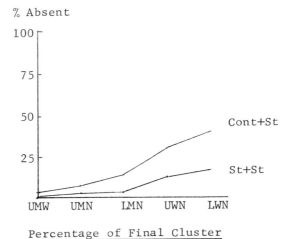

% Absent

Percentage of Final Cluster
Member Absent

	St+St	Cont+St
UMW	0.0	3.5
UMN	4.0	7.2
LMN	3.3	17.6
UWN	12.1	29.3
LWN	16.1	40.2

Fig. 12.   Comparison of Stop + Stop and Continuant +
           Stop Bimorphemic Clusters when Followed by a
           Non-Consonantal Environment: By Social Class

Loflin's position must be viewed in relation to the preceding description of bimorphemic cluster-final stops.   The
same type of pattern (except for relative frequency) is found
for both monomorphemic and bimorphemic clusters, suggesting
that there is a generalized phonological rule.   The effect
of phonological environment reveals the same type of influence

from consonant and non-consonantal environments for both types
of clusters. Also, there is a consistent difference between
the types of bimorphemic clusters (viz. stop + stop versus
continuant + stop) based on their phonological composition,
which suggests the operation of a phonological pattern. How
can one account for the difference in percentages found between different types of clusters based on phonetic composition
if a grammatical solution is chosen? Furthermore, there is a
reasonable phonological explanation (viz. compensatory lengthening) as to why the different percentages occur. Finally,
the fact that the absence of cluster-final stops is found not
only when the -ed form is associated with the past tense, but
when it is associated with noun modification (either embedding
or pre-noun modifiers) must be considered. Loflin (1967b:
12)[6] has suggested that the -ed form is obligatory in NNE
when associated with affixed verbs modifying nouns (e.g. the
scratched arm), but optional when associated with past tense
(e.g. Yesterday he scratched his arm). My analysis indicates
that the absence of the cluster-final stop patterns exactly
the same way for affixed verbs modifying nouns as it does
when associated with the past tense. The following examples
are representative of numerous attestations that when -ed is
affixed to a verb form modifying a noun, the final cluster
member may be absent.

It's a girl name Wanda (444:9)

A boy in my class name Rodney (489:29)

One can attribute Loflin's oversight in analyzing this
construction to his failure to recognize the phonological
pattern which operates on all forms to which -ed may be affixed. The phonological evidence is too great to choose a
simple grammatical solution. This does not mean that past
tense always occurs in NNE where it occurs in SE. The use
of -ed in NNE does, however, correspond closely enough to

its use in SE to make it quite clear that, in most instances,
the lack of cluster-final stops results from a phonological
constraint which causes -ed to be realized as zero (or,
possibly, to be realized in some compensatory way, such as
continuant lengthening).

4.1.4   Social Factors Intersecting with Social Class

Having described the function of monomorphemic and bimorphemic
clusters as they correlate to social class, we now turn to
other social variables which may intersect with status to
account for differences in speech behavior. These variables
include contextual style, sex, age, and racial isolation.

4.1.4.1   Style

At least two clear-cut styles of speech were recorded as part
of the questionnaire used by the Detroit Dialect Study, namely,
interview and reading style (see Appendix B). In measuring
the differences in stylistic variation, several restrictions
in the sample population must be noted. In the first place,
only the teen-agers and adults were given the reading passage,
since it was considered too difficult for many 10-to-12-year-
old pre-adolescents. Also, several of the lower-working class
adults were unable to read the passage because of inadequate
reading skills. Since some lower-working class informants
couldn't read the passage, upper and lower-working class informants are combined (abbreviated WN) in the comparison of
interview and reading styles. Thirteen informants represent
the working class, whereas eight informants represent each
of the other classes.

In Fig. 13 the difference between interview and reading
style are given for monomorphemic clusters, distinguishing
consonantal and non-consonantal environments.

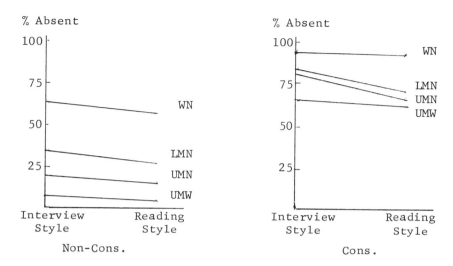

Percentage of Final Cluster Member Absence when
Followed by a Non-Consonantal and Consonantal
Environment

	Non-Cons.		Cons.	
	Interview Style	Reading Style	Interview Style	Reading Style
UMW	11.9	4.0	67.1	62.5
UMN	20.0	16.7	81.6	64.3
LMN	36.9	25.0	82.9	69.6
WN	67.7	57.3	93.6	92.9

Fig. 13.   Comparison of Monomorphemic Clusters in Interview
and Reading Style: By Social Class

In the non-consonantal environment the LMN and WN show
the greatest variation between the styles. When followed by
a consonant it is the UMN and LMN classes which show the
greatest stylistic variation. Both of these classes closely
approximate the figures for UMW in the reading style. In
the interview UMN and LMN show a considerably higher percentage of absence.

In reference to the bimorphemic clusters, shown in
Fig. 14, the WN indicates the most stylistic variation in

the non-consonantal environment and the UMW and LMN classes
indicate the greatest stylistic variation when followed by a
consonant.

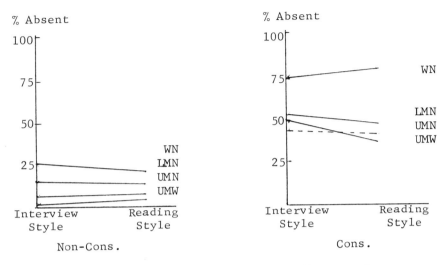

Percentage of Final Cluster Member Absence when
Followed by a Non-Consonantal and Consonantal
Environment

	Non-Cons.		Cons.	
	Interview Style	Reading Style	Interview Style	Reading Style
UMW	1.4	2.5	50.0	37.2
UMN	5.3	5.0	46.5	43.8
LMN	14.9	12.5	56.6	48.9
WN	25.2	19.0	75.0	78.7

Fig. 14. Comparison of Bimorphemic Clusters in Interview
          and Reading Style: By Social Class

4.1.4.2 Sex

Exploratory analysis on the data collected by the Detroit
Dialect Study (Shuy, Wolfram and Riley 1967) has suggested
that females show a greater sensitivity to socially evalu-
ative linguistic features than do males. If this is

applicable to the consonant cluster index, one can expect to
find consistently lower percentages of cluster-final stop
absence for the female population. Taking the most socially
diagnostic environments for monomorphemic and bimorphemic
clusters, namely, when followed by a non-consonantal environment, the male and female percentages are given for each
social class in Fig. 15. Six informants of each sex are
represented in each social class.

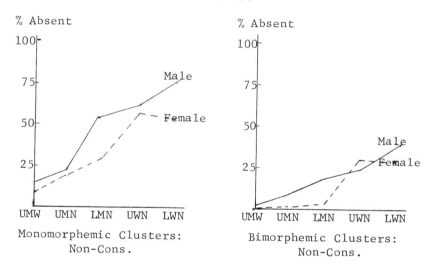

Monomorphemic Clusters: Bimorphemic Clusters:
      Non-Cons.   Non-Cons.

Percentage of Final Cluster Member Absence
in Monomorphemic and Bimorphemic Clusters

	Monomorphemic		Bimorphemic	
	Male	Female	Male	Female
UMW	14.8	8.2	5.7	0.0
UMN	23.3	21.9	10.3	3.4
LMN	57.6	30.9	17.5	7.3
UWN	67.1	63.5	24.5	27.3
LWN	79.1	55.6	39.0	28.8

Fig. 15.   Absence of Final Cluster Member in Monomorphemic
           and Bimorphemic Clusters when Followed by a Non-
           Consonantal Environment: By Social Class and Sex

Fig. 15 indicates that only in one instance (bimorphemic clusters for the UWN class) do the females show a greater percentage of absence than the males. In all remaining instances, the females seem to show a greater awareness of the social consequences of cluster-final absence. If the totals for the 24 Negro females of all social classes are compared with the totals for the 24 males of all social classes, the male percentage of absence exceeds the females' by 14 per cent (57.8 to 43.7) for monomorphemic clusters and by 5 per cent (22.9 to 17.8) for bimorphemic clusters. The greatest difference between the sexes is found between the LMN males and females.

Fig. 15 does suggest that the distinction of sex is a factor intersecting with social status to account for differences in speech behavior.

4.1.4.3 Age

As was discussed earlier (see sec. 1.4.1), the sample was divided into three different age levels in order to observe the possible effect of age on socially diagnostic linguistic indices. The three age levels -- 10-to-12-year-old pre-adolescents, 14-to-17-year-old teen-agers, and 30-to-55-year-old adults -- were represented by four informants in each of the social classes. Although the number of informants representing each level is low, ages and/or social groups can be combined if initial quantitative results indicate age to be an important parameter intersecting with other social variables. In Fig. 16 the absence of cluster-final stops is measured for the three age levels.

Although Fig. 16 does not conclusively indicate the same pattern of age differentiation for all social classes, several things stand out. For the bimorphemic clusters, the relative frequency of final stop absence is generally higher for the pre-adolescents than either the teen-agers or adults.

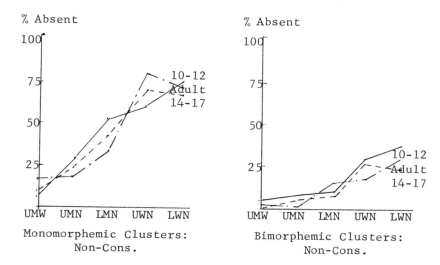

Percentage of Final Cluster Member Absence
in Monomorphemic and Bimorphemic Clusters

| | Monomorphemic | | | | Bimorphemic | | |
	10-12	Age 14-17	Adult		10-12	Age 14-17	Adult
UMW	7.9	9.5	14.3		5.6	0.0	2.9
UMN	26.5	23.3	17.8		9.5	8.5	2.6
LMN	53.5	43.2	31.9		12.5	11.6	15.2
UWN	61.2	71.4	79.2		33.3	29.0	17.8
LWN	75.0	66.7	74.4		41.9	26.8	32.5

Fig. 16. Absence of Final Cluster Member in Monomorphemic
          and Bimorphemic Clusters when Followed by a Non-
          Consonantal Environment: By Social Class and Age

The SE (UMW) and UMN adult informants show virtually no difference in their frequencies. The pattern for the monomorphemic clusters indicates that, for the Negro middle class
(UMN and LMN), the pre-adolescents have a higher frequency
of absence than the teen-agers, and the teen-agers a higher
frequency than the adults. The same does not hold true for
the working-class informants, who show little patterned age
differentiation.

4.1.4.4 Racial Isolation

On the basis of peer group isolation, supported by educational/
occupational and residency isolation (see sec. 2.2), six informants separate themselves from the rest of the informants
with relation to the extent of their contact with white peers.
These include two pre-adolescents, a teen-ager, and three
adults. The peers of these informants are either predominantly white or integrated between Negro and white. Five of
these are classified on the social scale as UMN and one as
LMN. Since it turns out that the racial isolation variable
is applicable mainly to the UMN class, it is relevant to compare only three groups, namely, upper-middle class white informants, upper-middle class Negroes with mixed or majority
white peers (abbreviated UMN_w), and upper-middle class Negroes
with majority Negro peers (abbreviated UMN_n). The number of
informants in each of these groups is 12, 7, and 6, respectively. These three groups are compared in Fig. 17, based
only on the frequency of final stop absence in a non-
consonantal environment.

An important difference is observed with regard to
racial isolation. The UMN_w informants approximate the figure for UMW informants, but the UMN_n informants show considerable difference from the UMW class in the frequency of
final stop absence. Two pre-adolescents and one teen-age
informant in this group mainly account for this difference
(for these three informants the percentage of final stop
absence is 24 per cent for bimorphemic and 45 per cent for
monomorphemic clusters). The adults do not show any significant difference from the UMN adults with predominantly Negro
peers.

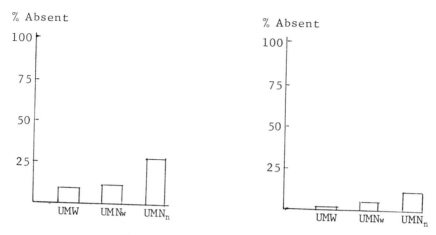

Percentage of Final Cluster
Member Absent in Monomorphemic
and Bimorphemic Clusters

	Monomor-phemic	Bimor-phemic
UMW	11.0	2.7
UMN$_w$	12.5	3.8
UMN$_n$	29.0	11.8

Fig. 17. Absence of Final Cluster Member in Monomorphemic and Bimorphemic Clusters When Followed by a Non-Consonantal Environment: By Racial Isolation

4.1.5 Summary

From the above description of word-final consonant clusters, several conclusions are apparent. The absence of a final stop in potential consonant clusters correlates with social class for both monomorphemic and bimorphemic clusters. The difference between the Negro classes appear to be largely quantitative for monomorphemic clusters. With respect to bimorphemic clusters, in the non-consonantal environment, the UMN class seems to differ qualitatively from the other

classes; the other classes differ from each other quantita-
tively. The factors of style, sex, age, and racial isolation
all intersect with social class. In addition to the extra-
linguistic constraints on variability, there are also independent linguistic constraints on the frequency of final stop
absence. The two most important linguistic constraints are
whether or not the potential cluster is monomorphemic or
bimorphemic and the distinction between following non-
consonantal and consonantal environments.

Although some working-class speakers show very high
frequencies of cluster-final stop absence in word-final
position, the effect of suffixes beginning with vowels indicates that there is an underlying cluster for most NNE speakers
which is most frequently realized as zero when word final.

The same phonological pattern operates on both monomorphemic and bimorphemic clusters, differing only in relative frequency. The reasons for maintaining that a basic
phonological pattern operates on both monomorphemic and bimorphemic clusters include:

(1)   The same general effect of phonological environment
      on variability operates for monomorphemic and bi-
      morphemic clusters.

(2)   Differences in frequency are based on the phonological
      composition of the cluster.

(3)   The operation of the pattern on -ed clusters is con-
      sistent, regardless of the grammatical function of the
      form (e.g. past tense, noun modification).

4.2   Morpheme-Medial and Final θ

4.2.1   General Procedures

The interdental fricatives represented orthographically by
th in SE (e.g. smooth, tooth, brother, nothing) are often
realized by labio-dental fricatives among some Negro speakers
([v] corresponding to [ð], and [f] to [θ]). In addition,

several other variants correspond to SE [θ] and [ð], including
[t], [d], and ∅ (i.e. no consonantal realization). In this
analysis, we shall limit ourselves to the correspondences for
SE [θ]. Four relevant categories of variants for the θ variable are distinguished as follows:

Category	Phonetic Realizations	Examples
θ	[θ] [tθ]	[tʰuθ] ~ [tʰutθ] 'tooth'
		[nəθɨŋ] 'nothing'
f	[f]	[tʰuf] 'tooth'
		[nəfɨn] 'nothing'
t	[tˀ] [ʔ] [t̆]	[nətˀŋ̩] ~ [nəʔŋ̩] 'nothing'
		[wɪt̆ɨm] 'with 'em'
∅		[wɪ≠mi] 'with me'
		[nəɨn] 'nothing'

Distributionally, these variants are largely restricted
to morpheme-medial and final positions. Morpheme initially
SE [θ] predominantly corresponds to [θ] among working-class
Negro speakers. For example, the morpheme initial θ in
thought or everything (i.e. every + thing) is found for both
SE and working-class Negro speakers. We are not dealing with
a basic difference in the phonemic inventory, but a difference in the environments in which [θ] may be realized.[7]

In measuring this variable the following procedures for
tabulation were adopted:[8]

(1) Beginning with Section I B of the interview, the first
15 instances in which θ might occur (i.e. "potential θ")
in morpheme-medial or final position were tabulated for
each informant.

(2) If the same word occurred more than three times, only
the first three examples were taken for tabulation.

(3) When potential θ was contiguous to a sibilant it was
not tabulated, since there is a regular assimilation
process operating in this environment regardless of
social class (e.g. [sɪks] 'sixth', [maw≠sət] 'mouth
shut').

Because potential θ does not occur as frequently as some
other phonological variables, less than 15 instances were
tabulated for several of the informants. The mean number of
potential occurrences of θ was 13.3 per informant.

4.2.2 The Correlation of the θ Variable with Social Class
In Fig. 18 the percentage of f, t, and ∅ realization for
potential θ is given for morpheme medial and final position.

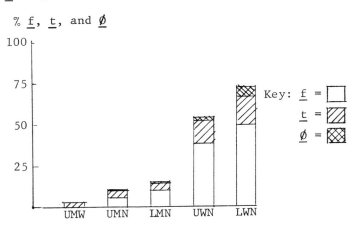

Percentage of f, t, and ∅ Realization

	f	t	∅	Total	Median
UMW	0.0	2.3	0.0	2.3	0.0
UMN	5.5	6.1	.6	12.1	10.0
LMN	11.0	5.8	.6	17.4	15.0
UMN	37.9	19.5	1.8	59.2	54.4
LWN	44.7	20.0	6.6	71.3	79.5

Fig. 18.   Percentage of f, t, and ∅ Realization
           for θ Variable: By Social Class

One immediately notices that the f and ∅ realization
are not found in the SE (UMW) sample. For the UMW, the
realization t is only found with the lexical item with.
There is a qualitative absence of the f variant for SE

speakers.[9] Because of the very low incidence of _t_ and the categorical absence of _f_ and _∅_ for this group, all remaining tabulations in this section include only the four social classes of Negroes.

In Fig. 18 there is a contrast between the middle-class (UMN and LMN) and working-class (UWN and LWN), when the realizations _f_, _t_, and _∅_ for potential θ are combined. Furthermore, 14 of the 24 middle-class informants reveal a categorical absence of the _f_ variant. For the working-class, _f_ is the most frequent realization. On the other hand, _∅_ is consistently the least frequently occurring variant for all social classes. Only the LWN informants have more than 5 per cent _∅_ realization.

In viewing the social distribution of this variable, we have up to this point simply contrasted the realization of θ with all "non-θ" realizations (i.e. _f_, _t_, and _∅_). Although this is an adequate procedure in viewing the social stratification of this variable, from a linguistic viewpoint it is inadequate to combine three distinct categories of variants without investigating the possible influence of linguistic environment on the different realizations. One must ask if there are not specialized environments affecting the realization of particular variants.

In tabulating different variants of this variable, it is observed that two particular lexical items account for the majority of _t_ and _∅_ realizations. These are the items with and nothing, both of which occur quite frequently in the corpus. Since the variants which are realized are somewhat different from those observed in other items, we may look at these individually. In Fig. 19 we observe the relative frequency of different variants which occur in the lexical item with for the four social classes; in Fig. 20, the relative frequency of variants for nothing.

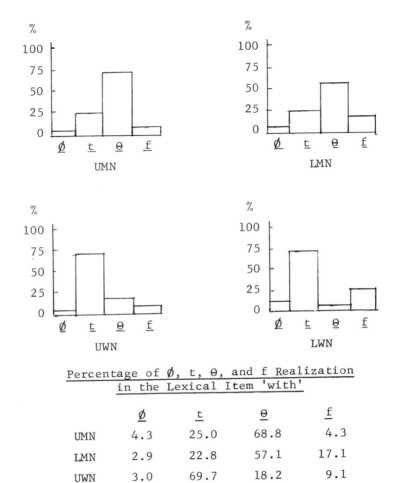

Percentage of Ø, t, Θ, and f Realization
in the Lexical Item 'with'

	Ø	t	Θ	f
UMN	4.3	25.0	68.8	4.3
LMN	2.9	22.8	57.1	17.1
UWN	3.0	69.7	18.2	9.1
LWN	6.1	72.7	3.0	24.2

Fig. 19. Percentage of Ø, t, Θ, and f Realization in the Lexical Item with:
By Social Class

Fig. 19 reveals that Ø occurs very infrequently regardless of social class of Negroes. A close examination of the
environments which follow when Ø is realized indicates that
these are largely labial segments (e.g. [wɪ#mi] 'with me',
[wɪ#wɜrk] 'with work'). The several instances of Ø can be
accounted for on the basis of its following environment.

Ø realization appears to have little or no social significance with the word with.

Fig. 19, on the other hand, reveals the very high frequency of t with this lexical item, especially for the working class. In fact, when this lexical item is excluded from the overall tabulation, the incidence of t drops sharply. What can account for the high frequency of t in the lexical item with? Is there some phonetic basis? One possible explanation is that the preposition with often occurs unstressed, which may affect a reduction from a fricative to a stop. Unfortunately, there are no other English prepositions ending in potential θ, so that this hypothesis cannot be adequately tested.

Fig. 20 depicts the relative frequency of the four categories of variants for the lexical item nothing, which also shows a pattern of realization different from other lexical items.

The realization of different variants for θ shows both similarities and differences with lexical item with. Like with, all four categories of variants are represented among the working class. For the middle class only t and θ are represented, the predominant realization being SE θ.

Of the non-θ realizations, we note that t again is the most frequent variant, although it does not occur as frequently as it does in with. In attempting to account for the incidence of t on the basis of phonological environment we note that the following environment is often a syllabic nasal (e.g. [nətⁿŋ]). Supporting evidence that the nasal is a conditioning factor in the realization of the variant t is found in other items in which potential θ is followed by a nasal (e.g. [rɪtⁿmətɪk] 'arithmetic').

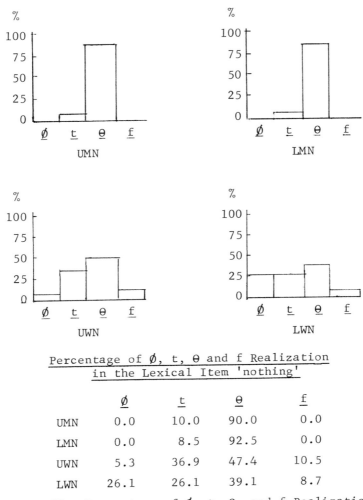

Percentage of Ø, t, Θ and f Realization
in the Lexical Item 'nothing'

	Ø	t	Θ	f
UMN	0.0	10.0	90.0	0.0
LMN	0.0	8.5	92.5	0.0
UWN	5.3	36.9	47.4	10.5
LWN	26.1	26.1	39.1	8.7

Fig. 20.   Percentage of Ø, t, Θ, and f Realization
in the Lexical Item nothing: By Social
Class

In the word nothing, Ø seems to be a legitimate variant,
at least for LWN speakers. Unlike t, however, the nasal environment does not seem to affect this since other items in
the corpus which are followed by a nasal do NOT generally
realize potential Θ as Ø. The only possible relevant environment which can be noted is that of word-medial position.

An occasional tendency to realize word-medial fricatives as
zero when preceded and followed by a central vowel is observed among some LWN speakers (e.g. [məɪ:] 'mother', [ənəɪ]
'another'. This general process accounts for the incidence
of ∅ in nothing.

Finally, θ in nothing (43 per cent) is realized more
frequently for this item among working-class speakers than it
was for the lexical item with (11 per cent). Is there some
phonological basis for this difference in frequency? Again
we notice the difference in the position of potential θ; it
occurs in final position in with and medial position in
nothing. In the original tabulation of the θ variable, shown
in Fig. 18, the difference between medial and final position
was not distinguished. If these two environments are distinguished from one another in the tabulation (excluding the
items with and nothing), an interesting difference in the
relative frequency of θ is observed among working-class informants. In morpheme-final position, θ is realized 31 per
cent of the time, whereas in morpheme-medial position it is
realized 63 per cent of the time. Furthermore, in morpheme-
final position, 7 of the 24 working-class informants indicate
the categorical absence of θ, whereas the same type of categorical realization is not found in medial position. Since
there is a general pattern in which θ is realized more frequently in morpheme-medial than in morpheme-final position,
the higher incidence of θ in nothing than in with is accounted
for on this basis.

In addition to the types of environmental conditioning
for different variants brought out in our discussion of with
and nothing, we may ask if there are any other environments
relevant to our discussion of the different variants. One
environment is that of a preceding nasal. When a segmental[10]

nasal precedes morpheme-final potential θ (e.g. month, tenth)
all three categories of variants are found. The incidence of
t and ∅ is the most frequent.[11] Of 11 instances of this type
of environment among working-class informants, t and θ each
occur four times. The incidence of ∅ is an extension of an
assimilation rule which we have already observed to operate
when the preceding consonant is a sibilant (see p. 83). In
SE, this assimilation only takes place when the following
consonant is a sibilant; in NNE, it may take place when the
preceding consonant is either a sibilant or a nasal.[12]

   A final environmental conditioning for the realization
of the t must be mentioned, namely, the possible effect of
a following stop on potential θ. In several instances, when
followed by a stop, the variant t is realized (e.g.
[mawt#klowzd] 'mouth closed').

   The above description of environmental influence accounts
for practically all instances of t and ∅ realization. In all
other environments, the variation is predominantly between f
and the SE norm θ.

   At this point in our discussion, we may consider the
implications of the previous description of variants on an
ideal construct of the NNE phonological system. There is no
consistent contrast between f and θ in morpheme medial and
final position in NNE. The fact that f is the predominant
realization in this position might cause one to conclude that
f is simply the realization of one underlying unit (i.e. the
morphophoneme F) and any occurrence of θ in this environment
is simply an SE importation. Fasold (1968: 3-5), from the
viewpoint of generative phonology, has suggested that there
are two underlying sources for the f which may be realized
in such words as off and with. His formal reason for asserting that there are two underlying morphophonemes which may
be realized as f lies in the fact that underlying TH can have

variants (particularly t) not permissible when the underlying form is F. Thus:

/git ɔf ma bayk/ 'Get off my bike'

/kəm bæk wif ma bayk/ 'Come back with my bike'

/kəm bæk wit ma bayk/ 'Come back with my bike'

are all permissible NNE sentences, but:

*/git ɔt ma bayk/[13] 'Get off my bike'

is not an acceptable utterance. The difference in the permissible realizations for these two utterances, Fasold maintains, can only be accounted for by positing two underlying
morphophonemes which may be neutralized in certain positions.
What takes place in NNE is a neutralization (i.e. element x
may be the realization of either underlying X or Y [see Lamb
1966b: 17]) of two underlying sources when f is realized in
morpheme medial or final position.

4.2.3 Social Factors Intersecting with Social Class
4.2.3.1 Style

No comparison of reading and interview style was attempted
for this variable because of the infrequency with which potential θ occurs in the reading passage. An exploratory
investigation of this variable in the first and second half
of the interview does not show any appreciable quantitative
difference between the two parts of the interview.

4.2.3.2 Sex

In Fig. 21 the percentage of f, t, and ∅ (i.e. all non-θ
realizations) is given for male and female informants in
each social class.

Fig. 21 indicates a consistent pattern of sex differentiation. In all four social classes, the females have
less f, t, or ∅ realization. The combined percentage of f,
t, or θ realization for 24 female informants is approximately

10 per cent lower than the 24 males (34.9 per cent $\underline{f}$, $\underline{t}$, or
$\emptyset$ realization for the females as opposed to 44.7 for the
males). The females come closer to approximating the SE norm
than the males do.

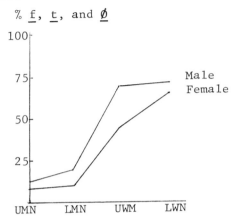

% $\underline{f}$, $\underline{t}$, and $\underline{\emptyset}$

Percentage of f, t, and $\emptyset$ Realization

	Sex	
	Male	Female
UMN	14.6	9.6
LMN	21.9	12.3
UWN	70.1	47.5
LWN	72.3	70.2

Fig. 21.   Percentage of $\underline{f}$, $\underline{t}$, and $\underline{\emptyset}$ Realization
for $\underline{\theta}$ Variable: By Social Class and Sex

4.2.3.3 Age

Fig. 22 presents the combined percentage of $\underline{f}$, $\underline{t}$, and $\underline{\emptyset}$
realization (i.e. all non-$\underline{\theta}$ realizations) for the pre-
adolescents, teen-agers, and adults. The three age levels
are represented by four informants in each social class.

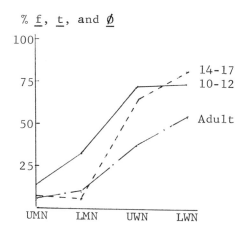

% f, t, and ∅

Percentage of f, t, and ∅ Realization

	Age		
	10-12	14-17	Adult
UMN	16.9	10.2	9.2
LMN	34.0	7.0	11.2
UWN	73.2	66.0	37.2
LWN	75.0	84.2	54.7

Fig. 22. Percentage of f, t, and ∅ Realization
for θ Variable: By Social Class and Age

Two differences in the above figures are noteworthy:
(1) the relatively high percentage of non-θ realization
among the middle-class pre-adolescents when compared with
the teen-agers and adults (combining UMN and LMN, f, t, or
∅ is realized 25.5 per cent for pre-adolescents, as opposed
to 8.6 per cent for teen-agers and 10 per cent for adults);
and (2) the relatively low frequency of f, t, ∅ for working-
class (UWN and LWN) adults (46 per cent, as compared with
the pre-adolescents 74.1 per cent and teen-agers 75.1 per
cent). Furthermore, six of the seven working-class informants
for whom θ is categorically absent in morpheme-final position
are either pre-adolescents or teen-agers (four pre-adolescents

and three teen-agers). The data reveal that age does intersect with social class to account for differences in the
observed frequency with which f, t, or ∅ is realized.

4.2.3.4 Racial Isolation

If the factor of racial isolation intersects with other social
variables to account for speech differences, one can expect
the middle-class informants with extensive white contacts to
contrast with the informants who have predominantly Negro
contacts. This is validated. The percentage of non-θ realization is 17 per cent for the group with predominantly Negro
contacts, whereas it is 7 per cent for the groups with extensive white contacts. One must note, however, that the greater
frequency of the group with predominantly Negro peers is due
largely to two adolescents who reveal 35 per cent f, t, or ∅
realization. If these two informants are in any way indicative of the effect of racial isolation, then racial isolation
has considerably more effect on children than it does on
adults.

4.2.4 Summary

Several conclusions concerning the social significance of the
θ variable are made on the basis of our previous discussion.
We have observed the sharp stratification of the SE variant
θ as it contrasts with the realizations f, t, or ∅. Among
working-class informants, f is the most frequent correspondence to SE θ. In terms of an ideal construct of the NNE
phonological system, a neutralization between the f/θ contrast takes place in morpheme medial and final position. The
realizations t and ∅ are restricted to several environments.
The variant t may be realized: (1) contiguous to a nasal
(i.e. a segmental nasal); (2) in the unstressed preposition
with; and (3) when followed by a stop. The variant ∅ is

realized: (1) following a nasal (and, as in SE, following a sibilant); (2) preceding a labial; and (3) a morpheme-medial position when preceded and followed by a central vowel. The incidence of ө among working-class speakers is greater in morpheme-medial than in morpheme-final position.

The factors of age and sex intersect with social class in accounting for observed differences in the relative frequency of variants. Racial isolation is important for the adolescents.

4.3 Syllable-Final d

4.3.1 General Procedures

In syllable-final position, when preceded by a vowel or constricted r,[14] the SE voiced stops b, d, and g (and to a lesser extent, all voiced obstruents) reveal several correspondences for some Negro speakers. Sometimes, a voiceless stop: p, t, or k (for b, d, and g, respectively) is realized. At other times, no stop at all (∅) is observed where b, d, or g might occur in SE. For my analysis, the voiced alveolar stop d, the most frequently occurring member of this set, is chosen for description. Three different categories of variants have been codified:

Category	Phonetic Realization	Examples	
d	[d],[15] [ď]	[hʊːd]	'hood'
		[hʊːďɔ́n]	'hood on'
t	[t˥], [ʔ], [ʔt˥][16]	[hʊːt˥] ∼ [huːʔ]	
		[hʊːʔt˥]	'hood'
∅		[hʊːbæk]	'hood back'

Generally, analyses of SE (see Trager and Smith 1951: 34) only recognize [d] and [ď] as realizations of the SE d phoneme. The unreleased voiceless alveolar [t˥], the glottal [ʔ], and the co-articulated glottal and unreleased stop [ʔt˥] are not considered phonetic realizations of d phoneme in SE. NNE

speakers reveal all three categories of variants corresponding to the SE phoneme d.

In measuring this variable the following tabulation procedures were adopted:

(1) Beginning with Section I B of the interview, the first
     20 instances in which syllable final d might potentially
     occur were taken for tabulation. The tabulation was
     limited to "content words"; "function words" (see
     Gleason 1961: 157) were not counted in the tabulation.
     Potential d was only tabulated when preceded by a vowel
     or r (potential d, when preceded by other consonants,
     functions differently and is treated under consonant
     clusters in sec. 4.1).

(2) If a word occurred more than three times, only the first
     three occurrences of the word were taken for tabulation.

(3) When followed by a homorganic stop (e.g. good tie),
     potential d was not tabulated.

4.3.2   The Correlation of d Variable with Social Class

The percentages of t and Ø realization are given for the four
Negro social classes and the SE white sample in Fig. 23.   In
the graphic display the shaded area represents the percentage
of Ø and the non-shaded the percentage of t realization.

Both Ø and t are found in all social classes, including
the white SE sample. However, the incidence of t and Ø among
the UMW sample is so infrequent that we may ask if it is not
an alternate realization for d in some quite restricted environment. A close examination of phonological environment
for SE speakers indicates that t only occurs in the unstressed
syllables of polysyllabic words (e.g. [həndrɪt˺] 'hundred',
[stupɪt˺] 'stupid'). The few instances of Ø are mainly restricted to environments in which a consonant follows (e.g.
[ga:məðɪr] 'godmother', [bulɪvar nirbai] 'boulevard nearby').

The Negro population does not show the same type of
environmental restriction as the SE speakers, particularly
in the realization of t. The variant t, for example, may

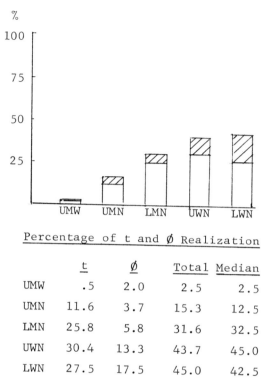

Percentage of t and ∅ Realization

	t	∅	Total	Median
UMW	.5	2.0	2.5	2.5
UMN	11.6	3.7	15.3	12.5
LMN	25.8	5.8	31.6	32.5
UWN	30.4	13.3	43.7	45.0
LWN	27.5	17.5	45.0	42.5

Fig. 23.   Percentage of t and ∅ Realization for
            d Variable: By Social Class

occur in items such as <u>bad</u> and <u>head</u>; it never occurs in these
items for the SE speakers. There is an important qualitative
distinction in the incidence of t for Negro speakers and SE
speakers. As far as the actual stratification of the four
Negro social classes on the basis of t and ∅ realization is
concerned, there is a gradient rather than a sharp increase
in the frequency of t and ∅ between social classes, suggesting that this variable does not stratify the population as
sharply as some other variables (cf. the θ variable; sec.
4.2). The minimal difference in frequency is especially evident for the LMN, UWN, and LWN classes, where a difference
of only 13.4 per cent in the realization of t is observed
between the three classes. For all Negro classes, the

incidence of t is considerably more frequent than the incidence of Ø.

At this point, we may turn to the possible influence of
phonological environment in producing the realization of t
and Ø among the Negro population. We have already pointed
out the importance of environment in observing the qualitative differences between the occurrence of t for the white
SE speakers and the Negro speakers. Elsewhere (see sec. 4.1),
the distinction between a following consonantal and non-
consonantal environment affects the frequency of particular
realizations. In Fig. 24 there is a similar type of environmental distinction, obtained by separating the following environment on the basis of vocalic versus non-vocalic environment. The vocalic environment includes any potential d
immediately followed by a vowel; the non-vocalic environment
includes any potential d when followed by a consonant or
pause of some type (either a terminal or non-terminal pause).[17]

An important difference in the frequency of t and Ø based
on the effect of the following environment is revealed in
Fig. 24. The incidence of t increases quite sharply for all
Negro social groups when the following environment is non-
vocalic. As far as the social significance of t and Ø are
concerned, the non-vocalic environment seems to be more
socially diagnostic than the vocalic environment. That is,
there is a greater discrepancy in the frequency of t and Ø
between social classes for non-vocalic than there is for the
vocalic environment. For example, between the UMW and LWN
there is a frequency difference of 40.6 per cent for the
realization of t in the non-vocalic environment, but only a
difference of 8.3 per cent in the vocalic environment.

In understanding the reduced frequency of t and Ø in the
vocalic environment, we note the actual phonetic realizations
of potential d when followed by a vowel. In SE, when a vowel

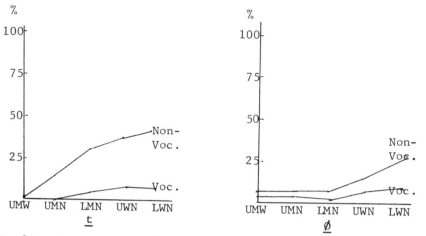

Realization of t and ∅ in Vocalic and Non-Vocalic Environments

	t		∅		Total	
	Voc.	Non-Voc.	Voc.	Non-Voc.	Voc.	Non-Voc.
UMW	0.0	.6	1.3	3.7	1.3	4.3
UMN	0.0	16.5	2.6	3.7	2.6	19.2
LMN	9.5	32.5	1.4	5.4	10.9	37.9
UWN	10.1	35.7	7.2	15.8	17.3	51.5
LWN	8.3	41.0	11.5	26.4	19.8	67.4

Fig. 24. Percentage of t and ∅ Realization of d Variable
in Vocalic Versus Non-Vocalic Environment: By
Social Class

follows the d -- particularly when preceded by a stressed
vowel and followed by an unstressed vowel (e.g. [raydɨr]
'rider', [lædɨr] 'ladder' -- d is realized phonetically by
flap [d̆]. In the Negro sample, the flap realization is also
found predominantly in this environment. Thus, where the
flap is realized in SE, it is also predominantly realized for
all classes of Negro speakers. In the non-vocalic environment, however, SE d often corresponds to NNE t. The low
incidence of t in the vocalic environment for NNE speakers
may be due to the fact that when the flap [d̆] is realized it
is difficult to assign d to the preceding syllable even

though it may be word final (e.g. bad apple, good egg).[18]
Rather, it seems to be ambisyllabic. Only when potential d
is clearly syllable final may t be realized for NNE speakers.

Having established the importance of the vocalic versus
non-vocalic environment in analyzing the variable, we may ask
whether there are other important environmental constraints
on the variability of the different variants. It is possible
to divide the non-vocalic environment into several different
types of non-vocalic environments. One plausible breakdown
can be made on the basis of: (1) a pause of some type
(terminal or non-terminal); (2) voiceless consonants; and
(3) voiced consonants. The delimitation of the pause environment is based on the impressionistic observation that
t appears to occur more frequently in this than in other
environments; the distinction between voiced and voiceless
consonants is based on the hypothesis that voicelessness in
following consonants may tend to influence that t realization
more than voicing. Fig. 25 presents the frequency of t and
Ø realization based on these three types of non-vocalic environments.

The most outstanding feature in Fig. 25 is the difference in the relative frequency of t when the consonantal environments are compared to the pause environment. A sharp
increase of t realization in this environment is found for
all Negro social classes. On the other hand, Ø is consistently less frequently realized in the pause than in the
consonantal environment. Thus, we see quite different effects of these environments for the realization of t and Ø.

An examination of the voiceless versus voiced consonants
on the realization of t and Ø does not show any significant
difference in the frequency of realization, although for most
social classes there is a slightly higher incidence of t in
the voiceless environment.

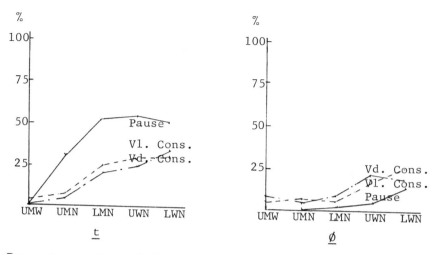

Percentage of t and Ø Realization when Followed by a Voiceless Consonant, Voiced Consonant, and Pause

| | t | | | Ø | | |
	Vl. Cons.	Vd. Cons.	Pause	Vl. Cons.	Vd. Cons.	Pause
UMW	2.2	0.0	0.0	2.2	5.5	0.0
UMN	12.5	11.7	34.4	6.3	4.4	0.0
LMN	25.0	22.6	51.0	5.6	8.1	2.0
UWN	29.7	26.0	56.3	18.9	20.0	4.7
LWN	30.3	34.1	51.2	24.2	18.2	16.3

Fig. 25.   Percentage of t and Ø Realization for d Variable
when Followed by a Voiceless Consonant, Voiced
Consonant, or Pause: By Social Class

It is possible to make more specific delimitation of
possible environments for potential d. Two different types
of counts were made just for the working-class (UWN and LWN)
informants. First, a distinction between the manner of
articulation was made according to three categories of environments, including: (1) a following stop; (2) a following
sibilant; and (3) non-sibilant continuants. When a stop
followed, t was realized 34.0 per cent, when a sibilant
followed, it was realized 17.5 per cent, and when a non-
sibilant continuant followed, it was realized 24.6 per cent

of the time. ∅ was realized 16.0 per cent, 35.0 per cent, and 21.6 per cent in the stop, sibilant, and non-sibilant continuant environments, respectively. The most interesting of these percentages seems to be the relatively high frequency of t̲ in the stop environment and the higher frequency of ∅ in the sibilant environment. With respect to the relatively high frequency of ∅, one notes an effect on potential d̲ when followed by a plural suffix -Z̲ (e.g. kids, boards). In 38 out of 53 (71.7 per cent) selected examples from the texts of several working-class informants, the realization was ∅.[19]

The second type of environment which was delimited was that of an unstressed syllable in polysyllabic words. The frequency of t̲ and ∅ realization in the unstressed syllable when followed by a non-vocalic environment was 54.1 per cent for t̲ and 28.8 per cent for ∅. The overall frequency of t̲ and ∅ realization for the non-vocalic environment was 38.4 per cent for t̲ and 21.1 per cent for ∅ for the working-class informants. For both t̲ and ∅ there is an increase in the unstressed non-vocalic environment.

We now consider how the realizations t̲ and ∅ fit into an ideal construct of NNE. Of particular concern is the status of the d̲ phoneme in syllable-final position for NNE speakers. We observe that the phonetic realizations [t˺], [ʔ], or [ʔt˺] are the same phonetic realizations which occur for the NNE (and SE) phoneme t̲ in syllable-final position (e.g. [bɛt˺]~[bɛʔ]~[bɛʔt˺] 'bet').[20] Before it is concluded that word pairs such as bed and bet, mud and mutt, and god and got are homonyms, we must note that these word pairs are still distinguished by the length of the vowel (and generally also a central glide) preceding potential d̲ (e.g. [bɛt] 'bet'; [bɛəʔt˺] 'bed'; [mət˺] 'mutt'; [məɨt˺] 'mud'; [gat˺] 'got'; [gaət˺] 'god'). How, then, are these realizations to

be considered in terms of a phonological construct of NNE?
One of the basic questions seems to be whether one chooses
to treat this problem on a phonemic or a morphophonemic
level.[21]

If one chooses to treat the apparently identical phonetic
realizations for potential d and t on a phonemic level, several alternate analyses are possible. One can maintain that
what appears to be an apparent phonetic similarity in allophones of the two phonemes is simply a problem of inaccurate
perception, and that in reality, the [t⌐], [ʔ], or [ʔt⌐] transcribed for potential d are different from the allophones
transcribed for the phoneme t. It is unlikely, however,
that the glottal stop [ʔ], for example, is any different
when transcribed for potential d or the phoneme t. Assuming
the two realizations are identical, one may choose to interpret the phonetic identity as a case of "phonemic overlapping"
If this is accepted as a case of phonemic overlapping in the
sense that Bloch, in his classic article (1941) has defined
the concept, this must be interpreted as a case of what he
calls "complete intersection" or "complete overlapping" between phonemes. Bloch himself eliminates this as a serious
alternative by noting that complete intersection is "always
the result of an error in analysis" (Bloch 1941: 281). A
third alternative is to consider the phoneme d in NNE distributionally restricted, so that it does not occur in syllable-
final position. If one accepts this solution, one must conclude that length is phonemic in NNE to account for the
contrast in vowel length which keeps bet and bed from being
homonyms. The conclusion that vowel length is phonemic has
some rather peculiar implications. Only in very restricted
environments do short and long vowels actually contrast.
Before ambisyllabic voiced consonants only long vowels occur;
before voiceless ambisyllabic consonants only short vowels

occur; before nasals in any position only long vowels occur.
This solution misses an important generality in the conditioning of vowel length and leads to a non-symmetrical
analysis of the NNE system.

The solution to this problem does not appear to lie in
an analysis on the phonemic level. Rather, it lies in the
morphophonemic description of NNE. What takes place is a
neutralization between two underlying forms (i.e. morphophonemes in syllable-final position). In syllable-final
position, t can be the realization of the morphophoneme T
or D. This solution allows for the general conditioning
environment for vowel length (i.e. voiced consonants) to be
retained while accounting for the occurrence of vowel length
before t in syllable-final position. In this way the basic
symmetry of the NNE phonemic system is not upset. Another
formal reason for choosing a morphophonemic solution is the
effect that suffixal -Z has on t and d (see note 18). When
the underlying form to which -Z is suffixed ends in t, the
t is usually retained (e.g. [bɪts] 'bits'), but when the
underlying form ends in d, the d is often absent (e.g. [kiːz]
'kids'). This phenomenon cannot be accounted for unless
two underlying sources for syllable-final t are recognized.

4.3.3 Social Factors Intersecting with Social Class
4.3.3.1 Style
In Fig. 25 the incidence of t and ∅ have been tabulated for
reading and interview style. Figures are given only for
three Negro groups, the UMN, LMN, and WN informants.

There is little difference between the interview and
reading style in any of the social groups. The UMN and LMN
classes show almost no difference at all in the two styles.
The WN class shows some stylistic variation, the percentage
of t and ∅ realization approximating that of the LMN class
more in the reading than in the interview style.

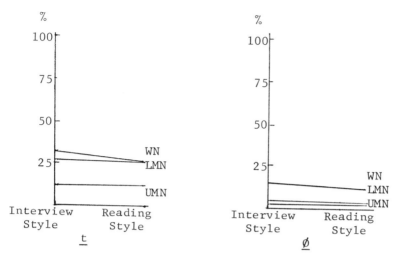

Percentage of t and ∅ Realization in Non-Vocalic Environment

| | t | | ∅ | |
	Interview Style	Reading Style	Interview Style	Reading Style
UMN	15.8	15.1	2.8	1.3
LMN	27.9	27.5	4.5	1.3
WN	35.4	27.2	17.3	8.7

Fig. 26. Comparison of t and ∅ Realization of d Variable
in Interview and Reading Style: By Social Class

4.3.3.2 Sex

The percentage of t and ∅ realization is given for the six
male and six female informants in each social class in
Fig. 27.

Although the incidence of t and ∅ is more frequent among
the male than the female informants, the minimal difference
in frequency can hardly be cited as clear-cut evidence of sex
differéntiation in the realization of t and ∅. (The frequency
of t for all males is 32.4 per cent and for females 31.0 per
cent. The frequency of ∅ for all males is 15.7 per cent and
for females 12.2 per cent.) The factor of sex does not seem

to have the same importance for this variable that it has for
other variables.

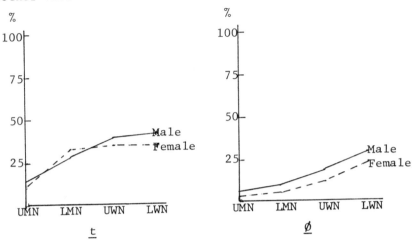

Percentage of t and Ø Realization in Non-Vocalic Environment

	t			Ø	
	Male	Female		Male	Female
UMN	16.8	16.2		7.3	4.4
LMN	28.9	33.7		10.8	4.8
UWN	40.0	37.6		17.4	14.1
LWN	43.8	36.6		27.4	25.4

Fig. 27.   Percentage of t and Ø Realization in Non-Vocalic
           Environment: By Social Class and Sex

4.3.3.3 Age

Fig. 28 presents the percentage of t and Ø realization for
the pre-adolescents, teen-agers, and adults.

A fairly consistent pattern in which the adults realize
t less frequently than the pre-adolescents and teen-agers is
revealed in Fig. 28. The teen-agers and pre-adolescents do
not show a consistent difference. The percentage of t
realization for all social classes of pre-adolescents is
37.6 per cent, for teen-agers 36.4 per cent. The Ø

realization does not show the same consistency in the differentiation between the adults and the teen-agers and pre-
adolescents, although the overall frequency of ∅ for the
adults (10.5 per cent) is somewhat less than for the pre-
adolescents (14.4 per cent) and teen-agers (16.6 per cent).

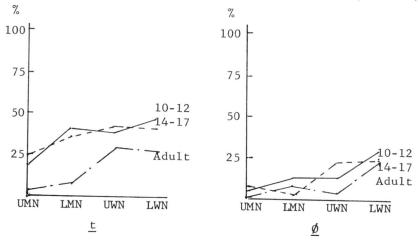

Percentage of t and ∅ Realization in Non-Vocalic Environment

		t				∅	
	10-12	14-17	Adult		10-12	14-17	Adult
UMN	20.0	25.5	5.4		7.3	7.8	1.8
LMN	41.8	39.7	10.4		14.5	1.7	10.4
UWN	37.5	40.4	31.7		14.3	23.1	6.3
LWN	47.2	40.0	30.2		30.2	25.0	23.3

Fig. 28. Percentage of t and ∅ Realization in Non-Vocalic
Environment: By Social Class and Age

4.3.3.4 Racial Isolation

The three groups compared in the racial isolation index are
the UMW (SE) sample, the middle-class Negroes with extensive
white contacts, and the middle-class Negroes with predominantly Negro contacts. As far as the realization of ∅ is concerned, there is little difference between the groups; the

UMW has 3.7 per cent $\emptyset$ realization in the non-vocalic environment, the UMN_w 4.8 per cent, and the UMN_n 6.7 per cent.
The realization of t shows a quite different distribution;
the UMW reveals 0.6 per cent t realization, the UMN_w 2.4 per
cent, and the UMN_n 25.9 per cent. For the UMN_n informants
it is two teen-agers (48.0 per cent) and two pre-adolescents
(36.4 per cent) who account for the differences between the
racially segregated and racially integrated groups. The
adults only account for 3.3 per cent t realization. Thus,
racial isolation has importance mainly as it intersects with
the variable of age.

4.3.4   Summary

In the discussion of syllable-final d variable several different conclusions have been suggested. These relate both
to the social significance of the d variable and the linguistic function of t and $\emptyset$ realization in terms of an NNE phonological construct. The sample population is not as sharply
stratified on the basis of this variable as it is for some
other variables. Social variables intersecting with social
class (particularly style and sex) are also not as clear-cut.

Linguistically, we noticed the effects of several different phonological environments on the realizations t and
$\emptyset$. These realizations are much more frequent in non-vocalic
than in vocalic environments. A more specific breakdown of
the non-vocalic environments reveals that t is more frequent
when followed by a pause than when followed by a consonant,
but the converse is true for $\emptyset$ realization. Following sibilants (particularly voiced sibilants) are also seen to effect
an increase in the incidence of $\emptyset$. Finally, the occurrence
of potential d in an unstressed syllable of a polysyllabic
word increases the frequency of t (and, to a lesser extent,
$\emptyset$).

The phonetic realizations of potential d̲ are identical
to the phonetic realizations of the phoneme t̲ in syllable-
final position. This apparent phonetic identity can be
described in terms of the basic NNE phonological system
either on a phonemic or a morphophonemic level. If one
chooses for a solution on the phonemic level, there are
three alternant analyses possible: (1) the realizations for
t̲ and d̲ phonemes, though appearing similar, are actually
phonetically different; (2) the phonetic identity should be
interpreted as a case of phonemic overlapping; or (3) the
phoneme d̲ is distributionally restricted (i.e. it does not
occur in syllable-final position); length, from this viewpoint, is considered phonemic in NNE. In my analysis, a
morphophonemic solution is preferred, maintaining that t̲ in
syllable-final position may be a realization of either an
underlying T̲ or D̲ morphophoneme.

4.4   Postvocalic r

4.4.1   General Procedures

One of the well-known phonological features showing regional
(see Kurath, et al. 1941, McDavid 1948) and social (see Labov
1966a) distribution in American English is the lack of constriction [22] in r̲. This lack of constriction has been observed when post-vocalic r̲ might occur in word-final position
(e.g. car, mother) or word-medial position when followed by
a consonant (e.g. barbecue, barking). In most cases in which
constriction is absent, a central vowel, either [ə] or [ɨ],
is present although there are few instances in which the
central vowel may also be absent (see Labov, et al. 1968:
101).

In tabulating this variable only two categories have
been delimited, the presence (either full or lenis constriction[23]) and absence of constriction. The following procedures

were adopted in measuring this variable:

(1) Beginning with Section I B of the interview, the first
    20 instances in which post-vocalic r might occur were
    taken for each informant. Only post-vocalic r either
    in word-final or pre-consonantal, word-medial position
    were taken for tabulation. Potential r which might
    occur with a contracted form (e.g. you're, we're) or a
    possessive form (e.g. their, your) were not taken in the
    tabulation (see sec. 5.3).

(2) In addition to the 20 instances taken in the above types
    of environments, three examples of potential r in word-
    medial inter-vocalic position were taken for each in-
    formant (e.g. marry, story).

(3) For the 20 instances of post-vocalic r, only the first
    three tokens of any particular word were taken; for the
    three instances of word-medial inter-vocalic r, only
    two could be the same word.

(4) When the following word began with r (e.g. River Road)
    potential r was not tabulated.

4.4.2 The Correlation of the r Variable with Social Class

In Fig. 29 the percentage of r absence is given for each of
the four Negro social groups and the white SE group. The
figures do not include the three examples of word-medial
inter-vocalic r.

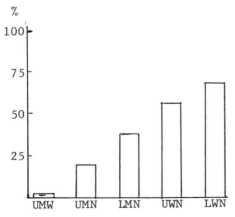

	Percentage of r Absence	
	Mean	Median
UMW	0.8	0.0
UMN	20.8	12.5
LMN	38.8	40.0
UWN	61.3	57.5
LWN	71.7	72.5

Fig. 29. Percentage of r Absence: By Social Class

The incidence of r absence shows a gradual rather than sharp increase in relative frequency as one compares the four social groups of Negroes. The white SE group reveals only rare instances of r absence. One may ask if there is not some specialized environment in which r absence occurs in SE. A close inspection of the environments in which r absence occurs for this group shows that absence is only found in unstressed syllables when potential r is followed by a consonant. The instances of r absence for the SE sample are so few that they can be limited to particular lexical items (e.g. [forwɨd] 'forward', [pʰətʰɨkyulɨr] 'particular'). For all practical purposes, we are dealing with the absence of r for a Negro community which is located within a regional "r dialect" area. (For analysis of r in a Negro community where the surrounding white community is also "r-less", see Labov, et al. 1968: 99-106).

Fig. 29 does not distinguish any effect of phonological environment for the presence and absence of r. For example, potential r when following a central vowel in such words as work, dirt, third [24] is included with all other types of post-vocalic r. But there are several different environments which affect the variability of r absence. In Fig. 30 three relevant types of environments are distinguished: (1) potential r in a stressed syllable when preceded by a central vowel (e.g. work, dirt, third); (2) potential r in stressed syllables when preceded by non-central vowels (e.g. car, four, hear); (3) potential r in unstressed syllables (e.g. mother, brother, teacher). Since the categorical presence of r as an SE feature has already been established for the UMW informants on the basis of Fig. 29, in Fig. 30 figures for the UMW informants will not be included in the tabulation.

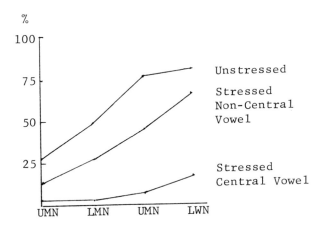

Percentage of r Absence

Stressed Central Vowel	Stressed Non-Central Vowel	Unstressed
2.6	16.3	28.8
5.7	30.6	50.0
9.7	49.4	78.0
19.4	67.7	84.4

Fig. 30.   Percentage of r Absence in Stressed Syllable
Following a Central Vowel, Stressed Syllable
Following a Non-Central Vowel, and Unstressed
Syllable: By Social Class

Fig. 30 indicates a sharp difference in the variability
of r absence based on these three types of environments.   The
incidence of r absence in stressed syllables following a
central vowel is so low for the middle-class Negro group that
one can say that only in isolated instances is r absent in
this environment.   Even among the working-class informants,
it is only 8 of the 24 informants who reveal any r absence
in this environment at all.   In an unstressed environment,
r absence is a rather frequent phenomenon.   Even for the
highest social class of Negroes, the incidence of r absence
in this environment is not uncommon.   For example, 7 of the

12 UMN informants reveal the categorical presence of r in
stressed syllables, whereas only 3 of the 12 show the categorical presence of r in unstressed syllables.

Up to this point we have not mentioned what has often
been considered to be the most significant environmental effect on the occurrence of r, namely, the effect of a following vocalic versus non-vocalic (i.e. consonant or pause)
environment. In descriptions of regional r-lessness, it is
generally recognized (see Kurath, et al. 1941; McDavid, in
Francis 1958) that a following word beginning with a vowel
sharply increases the incidence of r. In Fig. 31 the effect
of a following vowel on the incidence of r is observed. In
addition to the contrast between vocalic and non-vocalic
environments across word boundaries, three examples of word-
medial inter-vocalic r have been tabulated for each informant
(see sec. 4.4.1). The three types of environmental categories
are: (1) inter-vocalic, word-medial position (e.g. story,
marry) (_V); inter-vocalic, across word boundaries (e.g.
star on, four apples) (_#V); and (3) followed by a word beginning with a consonant (_#C). Ideally, each of these three
environments should be subdivided on the basis of the three
types of stress environments delimited in Fig. 30, but if
such a breakdown were made there would be too few examples
in each subcategory for tabulation. In Fig. 30 potential r
following a central vowel in stressed syllables has not been
included, since r absence in this environment operates in a
way that is significantly different from other environments
for the majority of speakers.

A general effect of the following vowel to increase the
presence of r is observed in Fig. 31. The absence of r when
followed by a vowel in word-medial position (generally considered to be present in all white r-less dialect areas) is
significantly lower than when followed by a vowel across word

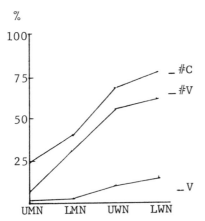

Percentage of r Absence			
	_ V	_ #V	_ #C
UMN	2.8	10.8	25.3
LMN	5.6	34.1	40.8
UWN	13.9	57.5	70.2
LWN	16.7	65.7	79.1

Fig. 31.   Percentage of r Absence When Followed by a Vowel
Within a Word, When Followed by a Vowel Across
Word Boundary, and When Followed by a Consonant
Across Word Boundary: By Social Class

boundaries. Labov, et al. have noted (1968: 101) that word-
medial inter-vocalic r tends to be lexically conditioned
(i.e. it only occurs with certain lexical items). Speakers
in this sample do not appear to show a lexical restriction.
Although Fig. 31 does show a patterned increase in r presence
for all social classes when followed by a vowel across word
boundaries, it does not approach the nature of a categorical
rule, which is sometimes claimed for this environment in the
description of regional r-less dialect areas.

Combining the insights made on the basis of Figs. 30 and
31, we may now say that the most likely environment for r
absence is in an unstressed syllable when followed by a word
beginning with a consonant (e.g. rubber gun). The least
likely environment for r absence is in a stressed syllable
following a central vowel and preceding a word beginning with
a vowel (e.g. fir outfit).

What are the implications of the above discussion of r
among Negro speakers for an ideal construct of NNE? Obviously,
a phoneme r must be postulated for NNE based on its consistent

occurrence in word-initial position (e.g. [rən] 'run', [ræp] 'rap'). There may be some question as to whether or not there is an underlying form (i.e. morphophoneme R) in post-vocalic position. In word-medial position and in stressed syllables following a central vowel, the quantitative evidence suggests that there is an underlying R which may sometimes be realized as a central vowel (or, in certain instances ∅). But in word-final position and word-medial position when followed by a consonant, the evidence is not nearly as strong, particularly when potentially occurring in unstressed syllables. In regional r-less dialects of American English, there is a strong case for postulating an underlying morphophoneme R because of the clear-cut morphophonemic alternation. (Before a vowel, r is realized; before a consonant it is often not realized.) Although several phonological environments affect the presence of r more frequently than others, none of these suggests the clear-cut pattern of morphophonemic alternation characterizing r-less regional areas. Thus, r may not occur in certain environments in the NNE phonological system. (i.e. it is distributionally restricted). Several working-class informants and one middle-class informant do not reveal any instances of r in word-final and word-medial position when followed by a consonant (i.e. in the 20 instances tabulated for these informants). It may well be that some working-class informants have no underlying R in these environments.

4.4.3 Social Factors Intersecting with Social Class
4.4.3.1 Style

In Fig. 32 the incidence of r absence has been tabulated for reading style and interview style. As with the analysis of style for the other variables, the informants are grouped into three social groups, UMN (8 informants), LMN (8 informants), and WN (13 informants). No environmental

breakdown has been made for the measurement of the two different styles.

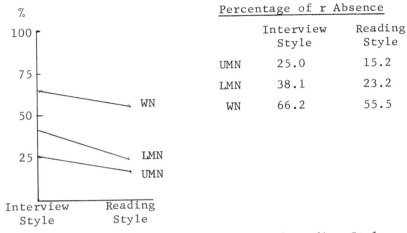

Fig. 32.   Absence of r in Interview and Reading Style:
           By Social Class

There is considerable stylistic influence on the absence
of r for all social groups. Of the three social classes shown
in Fig. 32, the LMN class shows the most variation between
the two styles (15 per cent), approximating the UMN figures
for r absence more in the reading than in the interview style.

4.4.3.2   Sex

Fig. 33 gives the incidence of r absence for the six male and
female informants in each of the four Negro social groups.
      There is a fairly definite contrast for the r variable
based on sex. Again we observe a pattern of female sensitivity to socially diagnostic features which is different from
that of the male informants.

4.4.3.3   Age

Fig. 34 gives the percentage of r absence based on the four
informants in each social class representing the pre-adolescent, teen-age, and adult age levels.

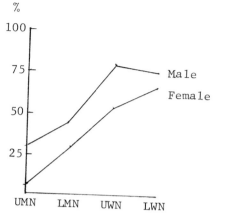

Percentage of r Absence		
	Male	Female
UMN	33.3	10.0
LMN	47.5	30.0
UWN	80.0	55.8
LWN	75.0	68.3

Fig. 33.   Percentage of <u>r</u> Absence: By Social Class and Sex

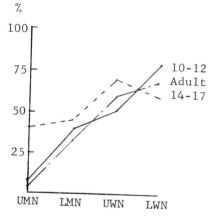

Percentage of r Absence			
	10-12	14-17	Adult
UMN	11.3	41.3	8.8
LMN	40.0	45.0	33.7
UWN	51.3	71.3	61.3
LWN	80.0	61.3	73.8

Fig. 34.   Percentage of <u>r</u> Absence: By Social Class and Age

A consistent age differentiation for all social classes is not revealed in Fig. 34.   The pattern of adult sensitivity to socially diagnostic speech features does not show up here as clearly as it does for other variables, especially for the working-class informants.   One explanation for the lack of age differentiation in the working class may be due to a social variable not considered here, namely, the fact that the majority of adults have migrated from regional <u>r</u>-less

areas of the South (all pre-adolescents and teen-agers included in this study were born in Detroit). Although no
adult informants included in this study had actually lived
in Detroit less than 13 years at the time they were interviewed, for the working-class adults, r absence is apparently
one of the more persistently retained features from their
Southern heritage.

4.4.3.4 Racial Isolation

The UMN_n informants have 30.7 per cent r absence whereas the
UMN_w have only 8.3 per cent r absence. As was pointed out
for the other variables, it is basically the pre-adolescent
and teen-age informants with predominantly Negro contacts
who account for the difference between the two groups. The
adult Negroes with predominantly Negro contacts show 10.0
per cent r absence whereas the pre-adolescents and teen-agers
reveal 39.0 per cent absence. Thus, racial isolation cannot
be viewed accurately apart from the age variable.

4.4.4 Summary

The Negro population shows a gradient rather than a sharp
stratification on the basis of the r variable. Several different environments affect the frequency of r absence, including stressed syllables following a central vowel, stressed
syllables following a non-central vowel, unstressed syllables,
and a following vocalic environment.

The r variable shows considerable stylistic variation
and sex differentiation, but age differentiation for the working class informants is not observed. Racial isolation, as
with other variables, intersects with the age level of the
informant.

As far as the function of r in an ideal construct of NNE
is concerned, there are some working-class informants for

whom an underlying morphophoneme R does not exist in certain
environments.

4.5 The Sociolinguistic Function of the Phonological Variable: Conclusion

Having examined the variables individually we may now turn to
some general conclusions about the sociolinguistic function
of the phonological variables discussed above. The discussion
can be broken down into two main areas: (1) the social factors
conditioning phonological variation; and (2) independent
linguistic factors affecting variability.

4.5.1 The Social Factors Conditioning Phonological Variation

On the basis of the independent description of the phonological
variables, several questions can be raised concerning the correlation of phonological and social variables. In the first
place, we may ask if the phonological differences between the
social classes are qualitative or quantitative? Are particular social classes in the sample characterized by the categorical absence or presence of particular variants or are the
social classes differentiated only by the relative frequency
with which certain variants occur? Our investigation of differences between the UMW (SE) sample and the four social
classes of Negroes have shown that a number of differences
are qualitative. Particularly as one breaks down the variables according to relevant phonological environments, differences which may at first glance appear to be quantitative,
turn out to be at least partially qualitative. For example,
although both the SE informants and informants in the four
social classes of Negroes reveal the absence of a final stop
in a potential consonant cluster when the distinction between
a following consonantal and non-consonantal environment is
made, it is only in the Negro sample that the absence of a

final stop in the non-consonantal environment is consistently
observed.

Determining the nature of the differences between the
four Negro social classes distinguished here is a more difficult matter. Certainly there are some middle-class Negro
informants who differ qualitatively from the working-class
informants with regard to the phonological variables described here. However, speaking for the classes as a whole,
the differences seem to be quantitative rather than qualitative. The θ variable is an exception to this observation,
since a majority of middle-class informants reveal the categorical absence of the f variant. Also, several of the
variables show a qualitative difference between Negro social
groups in certain restricted types of environments (e.g.
potential r when following a central vowel in a stressed
syllable; bimorphemic consonant clusters when followed by a
non-consonantal environment, etc.). But for the most part,
quantitative measurement is necessary to determine the correlation of these phonological variables with social class
in the Negro community.

Having suggested that the phonological differences between the four social classes of Negroes are quantitative
rather than qualitative, we may ask if the different phonological variables correlate with social class in much the
same way. In order to answer this question, it is necessary
to elucidate in further detail a distinction which has been
implied in our independent discussion of the variables,
namely, the distinction between sharp and gradient stratification.[25] By sharp stratification is meant a quite definite
break in the frequency of particular variants between contiguous social classes in the sample; by gradient stratification is meant a progressive difference in the frequency
of particular variants between the different social classes

in the sample.[26] These notions can be illustrated by means
of a graphic representation of the frequency distribution,
as follows:

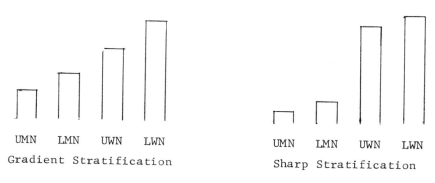

UMN   LMN   UWN   LWN   UMN   LMN   UWN   LWN
Gradient Stratification   Sharp Stratification

On the basis of the above distinction between sharp and
gradient statification, an examination of the four variables
shows that the θ variable is the clearest example of sharp
stratification in this study. The other three variables show
gradient rather than sharp stratification although in particular phonological environments variants sometimes show sharp
rather than gradient stratification.

The distinction between sharp and gradient stratification can also help us in our evaluation of the relative
"social diagnosticity" of a variable (i.e. the way in which
a variable serves to identify or distinguish a particular
social group). It is reasonable to suggest that the sharper
the stratification of a particular variable, the more diagnostic its function as a linguistic marker of social class.

Up to this point, we have only discussed the correlation
of the phonological variables with social class. But in our
discussion of the phonological variables independently, we
have seen the intersection of other social factors with class.
The specific variables seen to intersect with social class
are contextual style, sex, age, and racial isolation.

Each of the phonological variables for which formally
different contextual styles (i.e. interview and reading) were
delimited showed some quantitative difference between the
styles. This stylistic difference indicates that informants
recognize (whether consciously or unconsciously) that the
particular variable is a marker of social status. Both the
working class and the LMN class show more stylistic variation
than the UMN class, a fact which might be interpreted as
meaning that the UMN class is considerably more "linguistically
secure" than the other classes (see Labov 1966a: 93). Although
the UMN speaker may be more linguistically secure than the LMN
speaker, this observation should not be interpreted to mean
that the UMN speaker's linguistic security is equivalent to
that of the UMW speaker. The fairly persistent stereotype
that the speech of all Negroes is like that of the working-
class Negro causes even the UMN speaker a certain amount of
linguistic insecurity vis-à-vis the UMW speaker.

Suggestions in previous studies (e.g. Fisher 1958; Shuy,
Wolfram and Riley 1967) that females tend to use "socially
stigmatized"[27] variants less frequently than males are con-
firmed for the Negro speech community on the basis of these
phonological variables. The fact that sex differences in
speech are revealed for all four Negro social classes makes
it reasonable to suggest that slightly different expectations
in speech norms characterize male and female behavioral roles
on several different social strata of the Negro community.

Another factor intersecting with social class is age.
The way in which age intersects with social class is somewhat
different from what one might have expected on the basis of a
three-way classification. For most variables the speech of
pre-adolescents and teen-agers contrasts with that of the
adults. Teen-agers, even though they may show a greater
social awareness of the adult norms than pre-adolescents

(Labov 1964b: 91; see Shuy, Baratz and Wolfram 1969), do not
conform to adult speech behavior. The observation that teen-
age behavioral norms often come into "conflict" with adult
norms hardly needs elucidation. Although a teen-ager may be
fully aware of the adult norm of speech behavior, peer group
social pressure may cause the adult norm to be explicitly
rejected. To illustrate, one may note the following conversation, which took place when a fieldworker asked a 16-
year-old male informant how new members could be accepted
into his peer group:

> Fieldworker: What did he have to do to get in the
> group?
>
> Informant: He gotta hang around with us more -- come
> to visit; he have to talk cool, you don't
> understand.
>
> Fieldworker: How do you talk cool?
>
> Informant: Talk hip, man! -- you know. Like you
> don't talk like you supposed to. If you
> a square you can get out [emphasis added].

Before leaving the discussion of age, another way in
which age intersects with other social factors to account for
differences in speech behavior can be mentioned. In order to
discuss this intersection of age, it is necessary to discuss
two concepts relating to the frequency distribution of particular variants. The frequency distribution for informants
of a given social group may be described as being either
relatively fixed or diverse. By fixed frequency distribution
we mean that the informants in a given social group show
approximately the same frequency percentages for the different variants (i.e. the standard deviation score is minimal).
For example, if UMN adult informants show percentages of r
absence ranging from 5 to 10 per cent, one would say that
this group shows relatively fixed frequency distribution.
By diverse frequency distribution we mean that there is a

relatively wide range of scores for the informants in the given group. For example, if UMN teen-agers show a frequency distribution of r absence ranging from 5 to 60 per cent, one would say that the group shows a relatively diverse frequency distribution (i.e. the standard deviation score would be relatively high).

With the distribution between fixed and diverse frequency now in mind, we can apply these notions to the variable of age. The pre-adolescent and teen-age middle-class informants show a much more diverse frequency distribution than the adult middle-class informants. That is, the relative frequency of particular variants of a variable reveals much more fluctuation between individual pre-adolescent and teen-age informants than they do among adult middle-class informants. This characteristic of the pre-adolescents and teen-agers can perhaps be best illustrated by comparing the cases of two UMN pre-adolescent male informants (referred to simply by their tape numbers, No. 707, No. 726) and two teen-age male informants (No. 718 and No. 328). Their scores for the four phonological variables are compared in Fig. 35.

Fig. 35 illustrates the variance that is sometimes found for middle-class pre-adolescent and teen-age informants. One could maintain that the extreme cases are simply "atypical" examples which must be expected in any random sample, and that a much larger sample than the one used here would minimize the diversity. These cases illustrate a phenomenon which has been observed far beyond the scope of this limited sample, namely, that adult middle-class speakers are more likely to adopt middle-class speech norms than are pre-adolescents and teen-agers.

One can infer that as adulthood is reached, a more uniform pattern of speech behavior emerges among middle-class Negroes. Unfortunately, there are no longitudinal studies

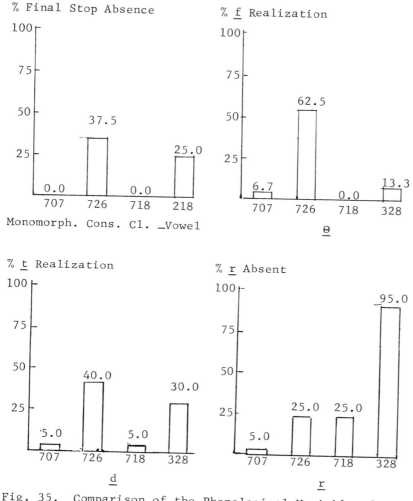

Fig. 35. Comparison of the Phonological Variables for
          Four Individual Upper-Middle Class Negro
          Informants

which can support this claim with empirical data. Among
working-class informants, the adults show a more diverse
frequency distribution than the pre-adolescents and teen-
agers. Working-class adults are more likely to adopt middle-
class speech behavior than are working-class pre-adolescents
and teen-agers.

The consideration of our final variable, racial isolation,
can help us account for some of the differences among pre-
adolescent and teen-age middle-class informants. The fact
that Informant No. 707 has predominantly white contacts and
Informant No. 726 has predominantly Negro contacts seems to
be the most obvious reason for the differences shown in Fig.
35. As has been noted by Hockett (1950: 449) "the most important environmental force shaping the emerging dialect of
a child is the speech of other children." Thus, the effect
of racial isolation should be much greater on the pre-
adolescents and teen-agers than it is on the adults.

Even though we have cited a number of variables which
intersect with social class to account for observed differences in speech behavior, there are variables which have not
been included here. No variable considered in this study can
be cited to account for obvious differences in speech behavior
between the two male teen-age Informants No. 718 and No. 328.
Both informants have predominantly Negro peers, both sets of
parents are from the North, yet there is a quite significant
difference in their speech behavior, as shown in Fig. 35.
What cannot be examined in a study of this type is the peer
group norms for speech acceptability, motivation for adopting
certain types of speech behavior, the social level of the
Negro peers, etc.

4.5.2   Independent Linguistic Factors Affecting Variability

In addition to our discussion of the social significance of
the individual variables, we have attempted to point out the
linguistic function of the variants in terms of ideal con-
structs of SE and NNE. For the most part, the difference
between these systems is not found in different phonemic in-
ventories, but in the environments in which these phonemes
may be realized. For example, both SE and NNE clearly have

/d/ in their phonemic inventory; however, the environments in which /d/ is realized are somewhat different for the two varieties of English. Furthermore, the underlying forms (i.e. the morphophonemes) in these environments are quite similar for SE and NNE.

There are various extra-linguistic factors which help us account for variability. But variability can also be greatly affected by linguistic environment. Both extra-linguistic and independent linguistic variables combine to account for systematic variation. For example, the systematic variation of r absence is accounted for by considering both the social characteristics of particular groups of people and the linguistic environment in which r may potentially occur.

The correlation of sociological with linguistic variables to account for fluctuation between forms has become well-established within the last decade of sociolinguistic research. But the notion of systematic variation as a function of independent linguistic variables has not been considered seriously. The fact that linguistic environment can greatly affect the variability of items has some important implications on the concept of "optionality" in linguistics. The limitation of linguistics to qualitative, discrete units has somehow precluded any effect that linguistic environment may have on variability. This is not to say that a statement of the relevant environments in which so-called "free variation" took place was not a requisite for adequate linguistic description. But the recognition that certain environments may affect the occurrence of a given variant much more than others was characteristically absent. Yet, each of the phonological variables discussed here has shown that certain types of linguistic environments intersect with extra-linguistic factors to account for variation between forms.

Recently, Labov (1968), who considers much of the variation between forms to be a matter of inherent variability
within the NNE system, has suggested that the notion of
linguistic and non-linguistic constraints be incorporated
into the formal representation of a linguistic rule.[28]
He has thus proposed what he calls the variable rule (1968:
24). By introducing the variable rule, Labov attempts to
formally incorporate the constraints (linguistic and non-
linguistic) which directly affect the variability of items.
To achieve this end, Labov suggests that "we associate with
each variable rule a specific quantity which denotes the
proportion of cases in which the rule applies as part of the
rule structure itself" (Labov 1968: 25). The value of a
variable rule is defined as a function of the constraints
which limit the categorical operation of the rule. This may
be represented as:

$$f = 1 - (a + b + c + \ldots n)$$

where f = the frequency of application, 1 = the categorical
operation of a rule, and a, b, c, $\ldots$ n the various constraints limiting categorical rule application (i.e. the
variable input). The constraints are "ranked" -- ranked in
sense that certain linguistic environments clearly outweigh
others in their effect on variability (e.g. $a > b > c > \ldots$
n).[29] For example, it is evident that the distinction between a preceding central versus non-central vowel in a
stressed syllable has a greater effect on r absence than the
distinction between a following vocalic or non-vocalic environment. Both have an effect on the variability of r
absence, but the effect is not equal. The relations of the
various constraints to one another may be viewed in terms
of a hierarchy -- each constraint in the hierarchy outranks
the effects of all constraints below it in the hierarchy.

Although Labov (1968: 30) has suggested that quantitative values can be assigned to the various constraints (based on the quantitative measurement of variation for a particular homogeneous social group), the calculation of these quantitative values is much less important than the fact that the general effect of these constraints is quite regular and uniform for the members of the given social group. Even though the actual figures for r absence may vary between speakers in a particular social group, the effect of a following vocalic environment in reducing the frequency of r absence is quite regular for all members of the group. This regularity causes us to formally recognize the systematic effect of linguistic constraints on variability.

What we have seen in our discussion of the individual phonological variables in this chapter is a delimitation of different linguistic and extra-linguistic constraints on variability. It is the intersection of these factors which accounts for the variation between different phonological items in a systematic and regular way.

NOTES

1. The underlying (sememic) construction for passives and noun modification may in many instances be the same.

2. The advantage of adding the scores together is that it eliminates the cases in which insufficient numbers are available for individual informants. In most cases where there are adequate numbers of examples for all informants in a social class, the scores are very close to the arithmetic mean score.

3. The most frequent pluralized item for tabulation was "desks", which was elicited in Section II A (see Appendix B) of the interview. The pluralized form from several informants was not elicited, so that the figures in the table do not add up to 60.

4. In a test specifically designed to investigate the effect
    of suffixes beginning with a vowel on potential consonant
    clusters, Ralph W. Fasold (personal conversation) reports
    that there is a small minority of informants for whom
    only the first member of the potential cluster is present
    (e.g. [fæsɨs], [rɛsɨn]). For these informants, one con-
    cludes that no underlying cluster is present.

5. Available data indicate that stop + stop clusters operate
    the same way, but there are too few examples in the corpus
    to give a representative percentage for each social group.

6. Loflin's example (1967b: 12) is <u>The dude, pushed from the
    chair, got into trouble</u>. He suggests that <u>The dude, push
    from the chair, got into trouble</u> is ungrammatical.

7. At times θ is realized as a lenis [t] in morpheme-initial
    position (e.g. [tʰɔt] 'thought'). Because of the occa-
    sional [t] realization in morpheme-initial position, it
    has been suggested (see Bailey 1968: 571; Stewart 1964a:
    9) that there is no /θ/ phoneme in NNE. The predominance
    of [θ] (or [tθ]) in this position for working-class
    speakers in this corpus suggests that /θ/ is present in
    the basic NNE phonemic inventory.

8. Special measures to insure the reliability of the tran-
    scription were taken, since the distinction between [f]
    and [θ] is sometimes difficult to perceive from a tape
    recording. First, a tape was made in which alternation
    between the typical types of variants was produced by
    another transcriber. There was no problem in perceiving
    the difference between [f] and [θ] from this tape. Then,
    four informants were randomly selected and the occurrence
    of the different variants independently transcribed. In
    over 90 per cent of the instances, there was complete
    agreement as to the transcription of the variant.

9. It is interesting to note that the f/θ contrast is a
    relatively late acquisition for most SE-speaking white
    children (e.g. six-year-old children will sometimes say
    /mawf/ for /mawθ/ 'mouth'; see Templin 1957: 51). This
    lack of contrast as characteristic of a late develop-
    mental stage in SE plays an important part in the
    "stigmatization" of the correspondence of NNE [f] for
    SE [θ]. White speakers hearing this correspondence will
    often interpret it as evidence of retarded speech develop-
    ment among Negroes even though it is a legitimate NNE
    adult norm.

10. If a nasal is realized as a nasalized vowel (e.g. [mə̃f] 'month') the effect of the environment is like that of the vowel rather than the segmental nasal.

11. William A. Stewart (personal conversation) has pointed out that sometimes the nasal preceding potential θ will be realized as a voiceless nasal (e.g. [məN] 'month').

12. It is possible that this assimilation pattern may also apply to other preceding consonants as well (e.g. [dɛp] 'depth'); however, no potential examples are found in the corpus.

13. Asterisk (*) is used throughout this research to refer to impermissible utterances or constructions.

14. Among working-class Negroes, constricted r does not occur very often in this position; instead a centralized vowel is realized (see sec. 4.4). Where r does occur, however, it has the same effect as the vocalic environment.

15. What is transcribed here as a voiced stop often fades into voicelessness.

16. Occasionally, an aspirated alveolar stop [tʰ] also occurs as a variant of this category. Its occurrence is quite infrequent and tends to occur only when followed by a pause of some type.

17. The difference between (a) consonantal and non-consonantal, and (b) vocalic versus non-vocalic in the tabulations is found in the classification of pause or terminal juncture. In (a), pause and terminal juncture are included in the non-consonantal environment; in (b), in the non-vocalic. The effect of pause operates quite differently for the d variable and the consonant-cluster variable.

18. The implication of this statement is that the division of syllables on the phonological stratum of language must clearly be distinguished from "word" boundaries on the morphological stratum.

19. When suffixal -Z (phonemically /s/) is added to words ending with voiceless alveolar t, this same realization does not occur (e.g. [bɛts] 'bets', [bɪts] 'bits', [bæts] 'bats'). A similar type of realization does,

however, occur when a selected class of words including
that, what, it are involved in contraction ([dæs]
'that's', [wæs] 'what's', [ɪs] 'it's').

20. In unstressed syllables the distinction in length is
often neutralized (e.g. [hə́ndrɪt˥] 'hundred').

21. This is only an option if one recognizes the distinction
between these levels as valid. From a transformational
generative view of phonology, one has no option since
the "classical phonemic" level is not recognized (see
Chomsky 1961).

22. Following McDavid (1948: 194), the term "constriction"
is used here to include "turning up of the tongue tip
(retroflexion...), retraction of the tongue, spreading
of the tongue, and any other tongue movements providing
friction during the articulation of a vowel".

23. Preliminary attempts to consistently distinguish and
codify lenis and full constriction had to be abandoned
because adequate reliability in the transcription could
not be maintained.

24. This statement concerning a central vowel refers to a
phonemic interpretation of the segment. The actual
phonetic nucleus of the syllable may simply be a constricted r (e.g. [wɻk], [dɻt]).

25. Although these terms may seem to show some similarity
of Labov's terms "sharp" and "fine" stratification
(Labov 1965a: 236), they are here used in a somewhat
different sense.

26. In an exploratory attempt to apply the "t test" of statistical significance (see Yuker 1958: 64-66) to these
notions, it was found that in the case of sharp stratification, statistical significance could often be
established for the frequency differences between contiguous social classes (e.g. LMN and UWN); but in
gradient stratification, statistical significance could
usually only be established between the frequency differences of non-contiguous classes (e.g. UMN and UWN).

27. The term "socially stigmatized" is used to refer to
variants generally associated with working-class speech.
Although it is the middle class which usually designates
a linguistic item as socially stigmatized, Shuy, Baratz

and Wolfram (1969) observe that the same attitude is often shared by the working-class speakers who use the variant.

28. Whether or not one treats the variation observed among NNE speakers as "inherent variability" or "dialect mixture" (see pp. 44-47), the recognition of independent linguistic constraints on variability is still essential. The position one takes concerning variation in terms of the two varieties of English does, however, have important implications for how he chooses to treat this variation in his descriptive approach to NNE. If one chooses to consider variants as dialect mixture, he need only talk about the effect of independent linguistic variables on dialect importations (i.e. a description of the inter-systematic relations); if he chooses to consider variants as inherently variable, independent linguistic constraints must be treated within the basic NNE system.

29. In the same sense that we suggest the ranking of the linguistic constraints, the effects of sociological factors can be ranked. Thus the effect of social class on variability may outrank the effect of age, but age may outrank sex, etc.

5 GRAMMATICAL VARIABLES

In the preceding chapter the discussion was limited to phonological variables. In this chapter, the social significance
of grammatical variables is considered. The variables will
be discussed, first independently, then as they relate to a
unified view of their social significance.

5.1 Suffixal -Z

In SE the suffix represented by -Z (orthographically represented by -s, -es, or 's) has several grammatical functions,
including third person singular present tense concord (e.g.
he goes), possessive marker (e.g. John's hat), and plural
marker (e.g. five dollars). Phonemically, -Z is realized
/ɨz/ following sibilants (e.g. /brəšɨz/ 'brushes'), /z/ following non-sibilant voiced segments (e.g. /gɪvz/ 'gives'),
and /s/ following non-sibilant voiceless segments (e.g.
/bayts/ 'bites'). Among Negro speakers, suffixal -Z is sometimes absent, so that constructions such as he go, John hat,
and five dollar occur. In this analysis the three grammatical
functions of -Z are considered both independently and in relation to one another.[1]

5.1.1 Procedure for Tabulation

Beginning with Section I B of the interview all potential
instances of -Z suffix associated with the third person
singular present tense concord, possession, and plural were

tabulated. For the plural subvariable, which is by far the most frequent of the three types, only the first 100 potential instances of -Z were tabulated; for the other two sub-variables, all instances were taken. There was an adequate number of examples of plural and third person -Z for tabulation, the mean number of potential instances per informant being 82.5 and 28.2 respectively. Possessive -Z is much less frequent and only 6.9 potential instances were tabulated per informant.

Two types of phonetic environments were eliminated in the tabulation because of difficulty in perceiving whether -Z was absent or present: (1) potential -Z when immediately followed by another sibilant (e.g. he tells someone); and (2) potential -Z when the base form of the noun or verb ends in an st cluster (e.g. he busts his hand).

5.1.2 The Correlation of Suffixal -Z with Social Class
5.1.2.1 Third Person Singular -Z

The incidence of -Z third person singular present tense concord absence is given for the four social classes of Negroes in Fig. 36. Since no clear-cut instances of absence are found among the UMW sample, only figures for the four Negro social groups are given.

The Negro social groups are sharply stratified on the basis of the -Z third person singular. Among the Negro middle-class informants (UMN and LMN), only scattered instances of -Z third person singular absence are found. Thirteen of the 24 middle-class informants reveal the categorical PRESENCE of -Z and among the remaining 9 informants, there are only 2 informants (LMN pre-adolescents) who reveal over 20 per cent -Z absence.

The absence of -Z is frequent for the working-class informants. Although its absence is relatively high for the

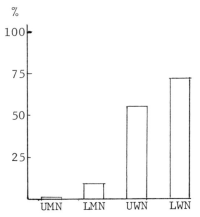

Percentage of -Z Absence		
	Mean	Median
UMN	1.4	0.0
LMN	9.7	1.6
UWN	56.9	64.8
LWN	71.4	73.6

Fig. 36. Percentage of -Z Absence in Third Person, Singular, Present Tense Concord: By Social Class

UWN and LWN classes, no informants show the categorical absence of -Z. In several individual cases, however, there are only isolated (5 to 15 per cent) instances of -Z, suggesting near categorical (i.e. "semi-categorical") absence.

To examine the possible effect of phonological environment on the occurrence of -Z, four different types of environment are distinguished for working-class (UWN and LWN) informants:

(1)   Potential -Z is preceded by a consonant and the following word begins with a consonant (C_# C, e.g. he talks funny).

(2)   Potential -Z is preceded by a consonant and the following word begins with a vowel (C_# V, e.g. he talks about football).

(3)   -Z is preceded by a vowel and the following word begins with a consonant (V_# C, e.g. he says too much).

(4)   -Z is preceded by a vowel and the following word begins with a vowel (V_# V, e.g. he says I can't go).

The percentages of -Z absence in these four environments are 62.4 per cent for C_# C, 67.4 per cent for C_# V, 72.2 per

cent for V_# C, and 61.8 per cent for V_# V. A clear-cut
influence of the surrounding phonological environment is not
indicated in these figures although there is a difference of
10 per cent between the V_# C and V_# V environments. What
is NOT found is the consistent type of effect of a following
consonant or vowel that was seen to be an important consideration for several of the phonological variables.

From the quantitative measurement, we observe that for
some working-class speakers -Z is much more frequently absent
than present. One may ask if there is an underlying (i.e.
lexemic) -Z in the basic NNE grammar.[2] Labov (1967: 163) has
suggested that this form is absent in the grammar of NNE and
that the infrequent occurrence of -Z is due to dialect importation from SE. Apart from the quantitative evidence,
there is structural evidence for Labov's view.

Structural clues that demonstrate a basic unfamiliarity
with rules governing the use of forms are essential in designating items as SE importations (see sec. 3.2). An important
type of structural clue for NNE speakers is hypercorrection
(i.e. the use of a speech form on the basis of a false analogy) of a SE pattern. Thus, in addition to the infrequent
use of third person singular -Z, it is observed that -Z
occurs with non-third person singular forms. -Z occurs with
all persons, as indicated in the following samples:[3]

First Person Singular

I plays that too (444:5)

I watches all of those (481:9)

First Person Plural

We plays in the street (193:35)

So we looks out the window (487:11)

Second Person (Singular or Plural)

... you goes places (193:558)

We had this test that you takes (461:1)

Third Person Plural

They jumps on her for nothing (318:26)

They heals up (370:17)

The incidence of -Z on non-third person singular forms
varies considerably among informants. For some informants
there are only isolated instances of this hypercorrection;
for others, it is common. Generally, the incidence of -Z
on third person singular forms is greater than it is with
other persons. When all occurrences of -Z with third person
singular verb forms are compared to its occurrence on non-
third person singular forms for the working-class informants,
-Z occurs over three times (233 out of 304 instances) as
often with third person singular than with other persons.
Only 3 of the 24 working-class informants have more occurrences of -Z with non-third person singular than with third
person singular. The data in this corpus do not confirm the
observation of Putnam and O'Hern:

> First and second person singular, and first, second,
> and third person plural forms regularly took the
> suffix s inflection while the third person singular
> form was uninflected. Thus, the verbs 'to like' and
> 'to go' were conjugated in the present tense, 'I, you,
> we, they, -likes; he, she, it, -likes'; 'I, you, we,
> they, -goes; he, she, it, go'. This usage alternated
> with the conventional inflection of the third person
> singular form and lack of inflection of the remaining
> forms; however, the conjugation described here is far
> more common (1955: 22).

These data indicate that, in most instances, -Z is
absent on all forms; sometimes it may occur on third person
singular forms; it also occurs on non-third person forms as
a type of hypercorrection. Of the occurrences of -Z on non-
third person forms, over half of the cases (39 out of 71
occurrences of -Z with non-third person singular forms) occur
with third person plural.

Occasionally, -Z also occurs on non-finite forms. There

are several examples of -Z occurring on infinites (He know how to spells big words (724:1)). There are also several instances of -Z occurring on other types of non-finite con-structions (including non-verb forms) so that examples such as I ain't sees him from 1928 (506:28) and I get rounds that crowd (506:28) have been found.

On the basis of the different frequencies with which hypercorrection is found for various types of grammatical forms, an important principle about the nature of hyper-correction can be suggested. There is a hierarchy of hyper-corrections which relates to the frequency of -Z. The number of instances of a particular type of hypercorrection is in-versely proportional to the degree of its deviation[4] from correct SE usage. For example, the most frequent occurrences of -Z among working class informants are found on third per-son singular forms, the next most frequent on third person plural. Usage with third person plural forms is more fre-quent than -Z with non-third person forms. Occasionally, but less frequently, occurrences of -Z are found on non-finite forms such as the infinite. This may be represented by the following hierarchical arrangement (> = 'greater than'):

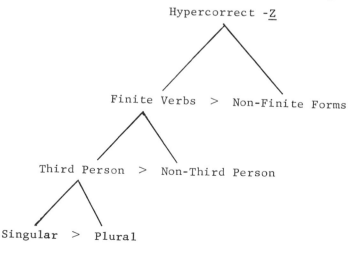

Hypercorrect -Z

Finite Verbs > Non-Finite Forms

Third Person > Non-Third Person

Singular > Plural

This hierarchy illustrates an important ranking of -Z
frequency based on grammatical form.

The fact that -Z absence occurs on a number of different
items, including possessives, plurals, adverbs, and the copula
(see sec. 5.3) might cause one to suspect that we are dealing
with a phonological rather than a grammatical phenomenon.
Such is not the case for a number of reasons. In the first
place, there is no comparable phonological pattern operating
on word-final /s/ or /z/ in lexical items (e.g. rose is
/rowz/ and piece /piys/) in NNE. Only when preceded by the
phonemes /k/ and /n/ is there any pattern of /s/ absence in
NNE (e.g. instance may be /ɪnstɨn/ and six may be /sɪk/),
but even in these environments /s/ is more frequently realized
than not. No similar type of pattern is found for -Z third
person singular. Also, the consistent effect of phonological
environment (e.g. following vowel or consonant) on -Z variability that was observed for the phonological variables is
not found for -Z third person singular. This is not to say
that phonological constraints may not intersect with grammatical patterns to account for variability between grammatical forms. If phonological constraints intersect with grammatical patterns, however, it can be expected that the phonological effect on variability will be of minor importance.

In anticipation of the discussion of plural -Z, we may
also cite the regularity with which -Z is found to occur in
certain types of plural constructions (see sec. 5.1.2.3).
This type of regularity for -Z plural would not occur if -Z
absence were a phonological rather than a grammatical phenomenon.

A final factor is the type of hypercorrection that is
found for this variable. Hypercorrection formed on the basis
of grammatical categories suggests a grammatical rather than
a phonological unfamiliarity with SE -Z third person. The

only reasonable conclusion is that -Z third person singular
absence is a grammatical phenomenon.

5.1.2.2 Possessive -Z

In Fig. 37 the relative frequency of -Z possessive absence
for the four Negro social groups is observed.

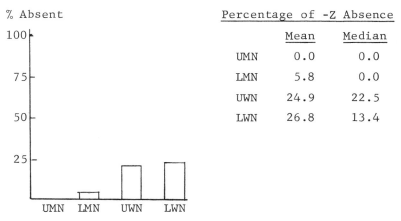

| | Percentage of -Z Absence | |
	Mean	Median
UMN	0.0	0.0
LMN	5.8	0.0
UWN	24.9	22.5
LWN	26.8	13.4

Fig. 37. Percentage of Possessive -Z Absence:
By Social Class

A sharp stratification between the middle-class (UMN
and LMN) and working-class (UWN and LWN) groups is indicated
in Fig. 37. For the UMN class, no instances of possessive
-Z absence are found. Only isolated instances of possessive
-Z absence are found for the LMN class. Although the incidence of -Z possessive absence for the working-class informants contrasts with the middle-class informants, the
frequency of possessive absence is considerably lower than
it was for third person singular -Z. William A. Stewart, in
a personal conversation, has suggested that the difference
may be due to the fact that the geographical origin of most
of Detroit Negro residents, the central inland dialect area
of NNE, has considerably more possessive -Z presence than
other Southern dialect areas of NNE.

The relatively low frequency of -Z possessive absence
for the working-class informants as a whole may seem to indicate that -Z must be considered an optional realization in
the NNE system. Although this is the case for most working-
class informants, there are several individuals for whom -Z
possessive is much more frequently absent than present. For
these informants, it is difficult to postulate an underlying
(i.e. lexemic -Z) as a part of their basic NNE system.

Several types of -Z possessive hypercorrection are found.
The most frequent type occurs with the item mines, so that
sentences such as the following are often found:

Mines doesn't sound like that (481:60)

I don't know how mines do (506:74)

The addition of -Z to this item results from an analogy
on the basis of the paradigm yours, his, hers, its, ours,
and theirs. Another type of hypercorrection occurs with
certain types of noun compounds, particularly those involving
proper nouns. This type of hypercorrection is illustrated in
the following sentences:

... they let me come home for Memorial's Day (565:54)

Well, there is Chrysler's Expressway ... (481:22)

A final type of hypercorrection can be noted even though
there are no examples of this in the data used in this analysis. This is the placement of -Z possessive on the first
noun of names involving two or more proper nouns. Hyper-
corrections such as Alvin's Jackson car for Alvin Jackson's
car are occasionally observed.[5] This type of hypercorrection
demonstrates a basic unfamiliarity with the SE grammatical
rules governing possessive -Z placement on the final noun in
compounds of two or more proper nouns.

The absence of -Z possessive, like the absence of third
person singular -Z, is the result of a grammatical rather
than a phonological pattern. As was stated previously, this

does not mean that phonological patterns may not intersect
with the grammatical pattern to account for some variability
of -Z absence in certain environments. An examination of
the different types of phonological environments (viz. C_# C,
C_# V, V_# C, V_# V) for the working-class informants reveals
that there is slightly more absence of -Z possessive when
following a consonant (34.6 per cent) than when following a
vowel (27.8 per cent). The greater frequency of absence
when following a consonant can be attributed mainly to the
nasal consonant /n/. Out of 38 instances of potential -Z
possessive following /n/, 15 (39.5 per cent) were absent for
the working-class informants.

5.1.2.3 Plural -Z

In Fig. 28 we observe the relative frequency of -Z plural
absence for the Negro social groups.

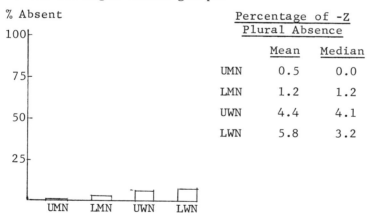

	Percentage of -Z Plural Absence	
	Mean	Median
UMN	0.5	0.0
LMN	1.2	1.2
UWN	4.4	4.1
LWN	5.8	3.2

Fig. 38. Percentage of -Z Plural Absence:
          By Social Class

Considering the total number of examples where -Z is
expected in SE, the incidence of -Z plural absence is very
low for all Negro social classes, even the working class.
For example, compared to the other -Z subvariables in Fig. 39,

there is an important contrast in the frequency of -Z plural
absence.

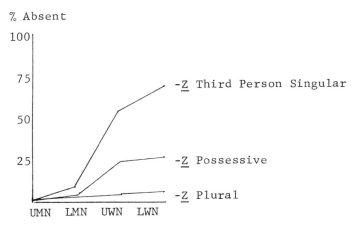

Fig. 39.   Comparison of -Z Third Person Singular,
           -Z Possessive, and -Z Plural Absence:
           By Social Class

In the tabulation of -Z plural absence in Fig. 38, no
different types of environments for -Z plural absence were
distinguished. Examples of -Z plural, where both linguistic
and non-linguistic context indicated -Z plural would be used
in SE, were counted. For example, given the sentence The boy
went to the show, there is no way of knowing that boy actually
has a plural referent except from the extra-linguistic context (e.g. the fieldworker asks the question: "What did the
boys do while the girls had their party?"). But given the
sentence, Ten boy went to the show, there is a linguistic
context (viz. the modifying quantifier) which indicates that
-Z plural would occur in this context in SE. Stewart (1966a:
64) has suggested that -Z absence is optional for NNE speakers
only when the noun co-occurs with a quantifier which is inherently plural (e.g. ten, many, etc.). If this is the case,
a significantly higher frequency of -Z plural absence should
occur in this environment. To test the validity of Stewart's

hypothesis for these data, the incidence of -$\underline{Z}$ plural absence when co-occurring with a plural quantifier was tabulated for the working-class informants. The quantifiers were divided between numerical (e.g. five, seven, etc.) and non-numerical (e.g. many, few, etc.) ones. For the nouns co-occurring with numerical quantifiers, -$\underline{Z}$ absence was 10.8 per cent; for the non-numerical quantifiers it was 6.2 per cent. A further analysis of the noun co-occurring with numerical quantifiers in terms of those which involve weights and measurements (e.g. inch, pound, cent) reveals 12.1 per cent absence. The higher frequency of absence for this category of nouns is due mainly to the monetary terms cent and dollar. For these two items, 9 of 15 instances of -$\underline{Z}$ (60 per cent) were absent for the working-class informants.

We have now seen that co-occurring quantifier and the type of noun does have some effect on the variability of -$\underline{Z}$ absence. It is noted that there is still 3.9 per cent of -$\underline{Z}$ absence for nouns which do not co-occur with quantifiers. Are there any linguistic factors which can help account for these instances of -$\underline{Z}$ plural absence, or are they simply random? Two minor effects, one lexical and the other phonological, can be mentioned in attempting to further account for -$\underline{Z}$ plural absence. Lexically, there are a few types of nouns, regularly taking -$\underline{Z}$ plural in SE, which characteristically do not do so in NNE. It appears that these must be categorized as mass nouns in NNE. Notice movie in the following sentences from working-class informants:

You know, like Saturday Night at the Movie (304:2)

We used to go to the movie often (583:4)

Where a consistent pattern of -$\underline{Z}$ absence associated with a single lexical item is found, -$\underline{Z}$ plural absence can be attributed to slightly different sub-classes in SE and NNE.

The one phonological constraint on -Z plural absence is
the preceding nasal /n/. It was previously mentioned (see
p. 140) that some lexical items potentially ending in /ns/
occasionally revealed /s/ absence. Occasionally (8.1 per
cent) plural -Z absence is found following a nasal (e.g.
/dɪrɛkšɪn/ for directions).

By citing the grammatical constraint of a quantifier,
possible differences in certain sub-classes of mass nouns
for SE and NNE, and the phonological constraint of a preceding /n/ we can account for most examples of -Z plural
absence. Of the few remaining examples of -Z plural absence
no clear-cut environmental effect has been observed (i.e.
they seem to be random). As far as the function of plural
in a NNE grammatical construct is concerned, it is evident
that there is an underlying plural -Z which may be realized
as zero in certain environments.

Several types of plural hypercorrection occur. The most
frequent type involves SE nouns that do not form their plural
simply by adding the -Z suffix. This set of nouns is small,
including such nouns as man, foot, child, ox, etc. Among
working-class speakers, these forms may be pluralized simply
by adding -Z (e.g. two mans (583:1)) on the basis of an
analogical formation with the predominant -Z plural pattern.
They may also be formed by adding -Z to a form already
pluralized by internal change, a suppletive form, or suffix
other than -Z. We find plural forms such as:

     ... two feets (193:38)
     ... two mens (208:66)
     ... two peoples (444:1)
     ... my own childrens (305:1)

The type of hypercorrection is observed in the speech of
10 of the 24 working-class informants. Less frequently, hypercorrection may involve the addition of -Z plural to certain

SE mass nouns, as in the following examples:

> ... <u>most of the times</u> (228:21)
> ... <u>watch televisions</u> (208:6)
> ... <u>good advices</u> (487:1)
> ... <u>watch TVs</u> (506:7)

The addition of -<u>Z</u> plural to mass nouns is less frequent than other types of hypercorrection in this corpus.

5.1.3 <u>Social Factors Intersecting with Social Class</u>
5.1.3.1 <u>Style</u>

Of the three -<u>Z</u> suffix subvariables, the quantitative differences between reading and interview style were computed only for -<u>Z</u> third person singular. Possessive -<u>Z</u> could not be tabulated because there were no potential cases of possessive -<u>Z</u> in the reading passage. For -<u>Z</u> plural the instances of absence were so infrequent in the reading passage that a quantitative analysis would not reveal any significant degree of -<u>Z</u> absence. Only four cases of -<u>Z</u> plural absence are found in the reading passage. Two of these occur in the

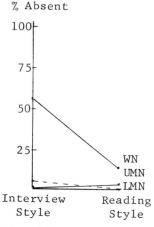

	Percentage of -Z Third Person Absence	
	Interview Style	Reading Style
UMN	0.9	3.1
LMN	3.6	0.0
WN	61.3	15.6

Fig. 40.   Percentage of -<u>Z</u> Third Person Absence:
By Style and Social Class

construction <u>the easy one(s)</u> and the other two in the construction <u>sixty time(s)</u>. Both constructions involve nasals,
the one with a co-occurring quantifier and the other without
a quantifier.

The stylistic variation of -Z third person for the teen-
age and adult informants is given in Fig. 40.

There is significant stylistic variation for the working-
class informants in the interview and reading style. The use
of -Z conforms much more closely to the middle-class norm in
the reading than interview style for the working-class adults
and teen-agers.

5.1.3.2 Sex

In Fig. 41 the percentage of -Z absence is presented for the
three -Z subvariables. For plural -Z absence, the tabulation
is restricted to environments in which there is a co-occurring
quantifier in the noun phrase.

The same overall pattern of female sensitivity that has
been observed for other variables is revealed in Fig. 41.
For the UMN class there is no sex difference in the frequency
of -Z absence, since -Z is usually present for all informants.
For the other three classes, males generally show a higher
incidence for all three of the -Z subvariables than the females.

5.1.3.3 Age

Fig. 42 presents the relative frequency of -Z absence by age.
As was done for the tabulation of -Z plural when the sex
differences were considered, only noun phrases with a quantifier were tabulated.

Of the three subvariables, -Z third person singular
shows the most consistent age differentiation. Pre-adolescents have -Z absence more frequently than both teen-agers

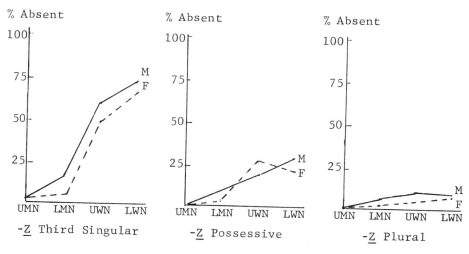

Fig. 41. Percentage of -Z Third Person Singular, Possessive, and Plural Absence: By Social Class and Sex

	-Z Third Sing.		-Z Poss.		-Z Plural	
	Male	Female	Male	Female	Male	Female
UMN	1.2	1.7	0.0	0.0	0.4	0.8
LMN	16.2	2.8	10.3	1.4	4.7	0.8
UWN	63.1	50.7	18.8	31.1	10.3	5.8
LWN	74.3	68.5	30.1	23.5	7.9	7.1

and adults, but teen-agers have more frequent -Z third person singular absence than adults. The data on the two other sub-variables are not as consistent, although a consideration of -Z possessive and -Z plural absence combining the different social classes suggests that adults reveal considerably less frequency for these subvariables also. The adult speech behavior fits a consistent pattern in which adults use stigmatized variants less frequently than pre-adolescents and teen-agers.

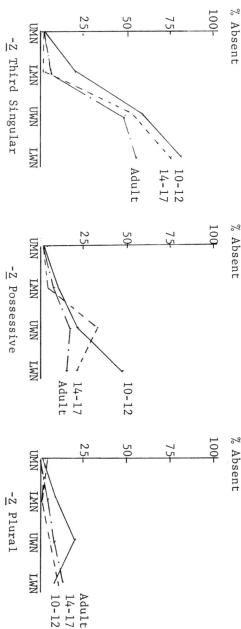

Percentage of -Z Third Person Singular, Possessive and Plural Absence

-Z Third Singular

-Z Third Singular	10-12	14-17	Adult
UMN	2.5	1.9	0.0
LMN	21.2	1.5	5.8
UWN	63.8	56.4	50.6
LWN	80.5	76.5	57.1

-Z Possessive	10-12	14-17	Adult
UMN	0.0	0.0	0.0
LMN	7.6	3.6	6.2
UWN	20.9	36.6	17.4
LWN	45.2	19.2	15.9

-Z Plural	10-12	14-17	Adult
UMN	0.6	1.3	0.0
LMN	7.0	0.0	1.3
UWN	17.2	3.4	5.0
LWN	6.6	7.4	8.6

Fig. 42. Percentage of -Z Third Person Singular, -Z Possessive, and -Z Plural Absence: By Social Class and Age

5.1.3.4 Racial Isolation

A consideration of the subvariables in terms of the UMN_n and
UMN_w groups does not reveal any significant contrasts. For
example, the UMN_w informants show 0.3 per cent -Z third person singular absence, whereas the UMN_n informants reveal only
2.4 per cent -Z third person singular absence. Furthermore,
neither group has any incidence of -Z possessive absence.

5.1.4 Summary

The sociolinguistic function of -Z suffix has been examined
in terms of three -Z subvariables: third person singular,
possessive, and plural. -Z third person singular is the
most frequent of the three suffixes absent. The absence of
third person singular -Z is a grammatical rather than a
phonological phenomenon, the basic NNE grammar having no
underlying -Z. This conclusion is based on quantitative
evidence and certain types of structural clues (particularly
hypercorrection) which indicate a basic unfamiliarity with
the SE rules governing placement of -Z third person singular.

We have also suggested that -Z possessive absence is a
grammatical rather than a phonological phenomenon. Although
the occurrence of -Z possessive is much more frequent than
-Z third person singular, there may be a minority of working-
class speakers for whom no underlying lexemic -Z can be posi-
ted. Several different types of -Z possessive hypercorrec-
tions have been noted, including -Z on the possessive form
mines, certain types of noun compounds involving proper nouns,
and the placement of -Z possessive on the first noun of names
involving two or more proper nouns.

The absence of -Z plural is much less frequent than -Z
third person singular and -Z possessive. Whereas it was
suggested that there is no underlying -Z for possession and
third person singular, there is clearly an underlying -Z

plural for NNE speakers. There are several environments in
which -Z plural is sometimes absent. When a noun co-occurs
with an inherently plural quantifier, there is a slight increase in -Z absence. With certain types of nouns, particularly monetary terms, the incidence of -Z plural absence
when co-occurring with a quantifier is fairly high. A slightly
different sub-classification of mass noun in NNE and SE also
accounts for apparent difference in the presence or absence
of -Z on particular nouns. Finally, there is an intersecting
phonological constraint (viz. /n/) which accounts for some
-Z plural absence.

The social stratification of -Z suffix shows the sharp
division of the middle class and working class, particularly
on the basis of the -Z third person singular and -Z possessive.
Other social factors, including style, sex, and age, intersect with social class to account for observed differences in
the use of the suffix -Z.

5.2 Multiple Negation

In SE, when an underlying negative element is realized in a
sentence containing an indefinite pronoun, determiner, or
adverb, the negative may be realized at one of several different places in the sentence. It is possible to realize the
negative on either the verb auxiliary or the indefinite (e.g.
He doesn't like anybody ⇔ He likes nobody[6]). When an indefinite precedes the verb, the negative is obligatorily
"attracted" to the first indefinite (e.g. Nobody likes anything ⇔ Nothing is liked by anybody). The negative attrac-
tion rule not only operates when any of the morphophonemic
alternations of not (i.e. /nat/, /nt/, /ɨnt/, /ɨn/, /n/) are
realized, but also with negative adverbs which are "inherently"
negative, such as scarcely and hardly (e.g. Hardly anyone
likes him).

Whereas the realization of a single underlying negative element takes place only at one place in most SE constructions,[7] in NNE it may be realized on every indefinite within the sentence. There is no restriction on the number of indefinite pronouns, determiners or adverbs on which it may be realized. Thus, in the sentence:

We ain't never had no trouble about none of us pullin' out no knife (583:21)

a single underlying negative element is realized at five different places in the sentence. The realization of one underlying negative at several points (basically a matter of negative concord) is distinguished from sentences in which there is more than one underlying negative element realized. Sentences with more than one underlying negative are indicated by emphatic stress on the second negative; these sentences naturally do not fit into the rule of negative concord. Thus, the sentence He didn't do nothing (as in the context He didn't just do nóthing; he was always busy at one job or another) contrasts with the multiple negation in He didn't do nothing (as in the context He didn't do nothing because he was so lazy)[8].

Multiple negation is a property of both NNE and white nonstandard English, as was noted in an exploratory investigation of this feature by Shuy, Wolfram and Riley (1967 Part III: 21-22). Although the previous study revealed quantitative differences between the use of multiple negation by NNE and white nonstandard English speakers, several types of multiple negative constructions not found among the white Detroit informants can be mentioned[9].

One type of multiple negation not mentioned by Shuy, Wolfram and Riley (1967) is the realization of a negative on a pre-verbal auxiliary in addition to its realization on an indefinite preceding the verb. We have declarative sentences such as:

    Nobody didn't like her (565:39)[10]

    Nobody can't step on her foot (444:4)

The occurrence of this type of construction among NNE
speakers fluctuates with SE Nobody liked her and does not
have a semantic interpretation different from its SE equivalent (i.e. Nobody didn't like her ⇔ Nobody liked her).

Another type of multiple negation found only among
Negroes is what has been called "inversion" (Labov, et al.
1968: 283) of the negativized auxiliary and negative indefinite in a declarative sentence. Thus one finds:

    Didn't nobody know it (214:15) = SE

    'Nobody knew it'

    Didn't nobody play in the sandbox (318:7) = SE

    'Nobody played in the sandbox'

The use of the auxiliary didn't in this construction
varies with the use of ain't (Ain't nobody know it). Modals
found in negative inversion include can't and won't. Frequently, the negativized indefinite receives an emphatic
stress, suggesting an affected or emotive meaning (see Labov,
et al. 1968: 286). The emphatic stress, however, is not
obligatory.

Although SE reveals inversion in imperative or inter-
rogative sentences (Didn't anybody come?), it is not found
in declarative sentences. Yet, the intonation and context
of the above sentences are clearly declarative. Informant
No. 318 uttered Didn't nobody play in the sandbox in response
to the fieldworker's question: "What did they have besides
swings?"

    And a sliding board, that's all -- and a sandbox.

    Didn't nobody play in the sandbox.

Labov, et al. (1968: 285) have suggested that negative
inversion is related to the negative auxiliary occurring with

a pre-verbal negative indefinite (<u>Nobody didn't like her</u> ⇔
<u>Didn't nobody like her</u>). The only difference between these
two, other than the emphatic nature of negative inversion,
is the linear order.[11]

In addition to multiple negation involving a pre-verbal
auxiliary, it is also possible to retain the same type of
construction (i.e. negativization of pre-verbal auxiliary
and pre-verbal negativized indefinites) across clauses, so
that sentences such as <u>It wasn't no girls couldn't go with</u>
<u>us</u> (= SE 'There weren't any girls who could go with us') are
observed. This is a simple transfer of the pre-verbal negative across clauses. The actual occurrence of this construction among NNE speakers is rather infrequent, although
Labov, et al. (1968: 267) cite several examples from their
study of NNE in New York City.

5.2.1 Procedure for Tabulation

Each incidence of a negative sentence occurring with an
indefinite pronoun, determiner, or adverb was tabulated for
the entire interview. The mean number of potential multiple
negative constructions was 15 per informant. The tabulation
included sentences in which the negative was realized in the
auxiliary (<u>He didn't do anything</u>), or in an adverb (<u>He never</u>
<u>does anything</u>, or, <u>He hardly does anything</u>). Not included
were examples in which it was possible to negate a pre-verbal
auxiliary which is preceded by a negative indefinite (e.g.
<u>Nobody liked him</u> was NOT taken even though <u>Nobody didn't like</u>
<u>him</u> is an equivalent multiple negative). The two main cate-
gories, realized (<u>He didn't like nobody</u>) and unrealized (<u>He</u>
<u>didn't like anybody</u>) multiple negation, were distinguished
in the tabulation.

5.2.2   The Correlation of Multiple Negation with Social Class

In Fig. 43 the percentage of realized multiple negation is
presented for the four Negro social classes and the white
social class used as the SE sample.

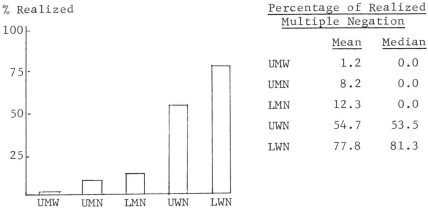

% Realized

	Percentage of Realized Multiple Negation	
	Mean	Median
UMW	1.2	0.0
UMN	8.2	0.0
LMN	12.3	0.0
UWN	54.7	53.5
LWN	77.8	81.3

Fig. 43.   Percentage of Realized Multiple Negation:
          By Social Class

A sharp pattern of social stratification is revealed in
Fig. 43.   The Negro middle-class (UMN and LMN) and SE white
samples show almost a complete absence of multiple negation,
whereas the working-class Negroes show multiple negation in
over half of all of its potential occurrences.   Labov, et al.
(1968: 276), in their investigation of pre-adolescent and
teen-age NNE speakers, have suggested that multiple negation
is realized categorically (i.e. it applies in all instances
of potential multiple negation) for genuine NNE speakers.
The categorical presence or absence of multiple negation is
presented in Table 13.   The operation of negative concord is
indicated by means of three categories: (a) informants for
whom multiple negation is categorically present, symbolized
by (+); (2) the variation between realized and unrealized
multiple negation, symbolized by (±); and (3) the categorical
absence of multiple negation, symbolized by (-).   Two types

of counts were made. The first count (referred to as the
"complete count") included all instances of indefinites in
negative sentences. The second count (referred to as the
"restricted count") excluded indefinites functioning "appo-
sitionally" to the central clause (e.g. I don't get restless
or anything) and the indefinite determiner a (e.g. He didn't
have a knife) since Labov, et al. (1968: 278, 280) have observed that these types of indefinites do not operate under
the same type of categorical rule as other indefinites.

Table 13

Categorical Versus Variable Operation
of Multiple Negation

	+		±		-	
	Compl. Count	Restr. Count	Compl. Count	Restr. Count	Compl. Count	Restr. Count
UMW	-[a]	-[a]	1[a]	1[a]	11[a]	11[a]
UMN	-	-	4	4	8	8
LMN	-	-	5	5	7	7
UWN	-	3	12	9	-	-
LWN	2	4	10	8	-	-

a = No. of Informants

There is a slight difference between the two counts.
Only 2 of 24 working-class informants show the categorical
operation of multiple negation in the complete tabulation,
but 7 categorically have multiple negation in the restricted
count. We may anticipate the discussion of age differences
(see sec. 5.2.3.3) and mention that the 7 informants who
reveal categorical multiple negation are either children or
teen-agers.

On the other hand, 11 of 12 UMW informants, 8 of 12 UMN,
and 7 of 12 LMN informants reveal the complete absence of
multiple negation. Although we observe that some speakers

differ qualitatively from others, there are still 22 of the
48 Negro informants who fluctuate between realized and unrealized multiple negation.

The relative frequency of multiple negation may be further analyzed according to several different categories.
Indefinite pronouns occurring in negative sentences (He didn't
hit nobody) can be distinguished from determiners (He didn't
have no toys). It is also possible to further analyze determiners into those including a in the count of potential multiple negatives (He didn't carry a gun) and those excluding
a (i.e. including only any as a potential multiple negative,
e.g. He didn't carry any guns). Another type of multiple
negation involves negative adverbs which occur either following another negative adverb (e.g. He hardly never comes home)
or in sentences where a negative adverb occurs with a negative auxiliary (The kids don't hardly come home). The four
categories relevant in observing the relative frequency of
realized multiple negation are: (1) negative adverbs (with
other negative adverbs or a negativized auxiliary); (2) indefinite determiner involving a; (3) indefinite determiner
excluding a; and (4) indefinite pronouns. The social distribution of these different types is given in Fig. 44.

Two observations are made on the basis of Fig. 44.
First, negative adverbs do not show as sharp a stratification
as the other types. The percentage, of realized multiple
negation is somewhat higher for this construction among the
middle-class informants than the other types. From this, we
infer that a construction such as The kids don't hardly come
home or The kids hardly never come home is a more socially
acceptable type of multiple negation (i.e. it is less socially
stigmatized) than a construction such as The kids don't do
nothing or He didn't carry no knife.

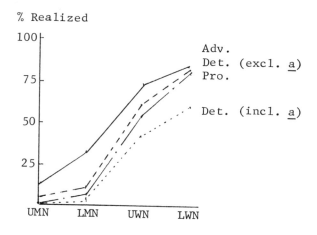

Percentage of Realized Multiple Negation

	Pro.	Det. (incl. a)	Det. (excl. a)	Adv.
UMN	4.3	0.0	0.0	15.0
LMN	9.1	2.0	3.1	32.0
UWN	56.4	39.1	51.9	73.3
LWN	78.7	63.5	82.5	84.6

Fig. 44. Percentage of Realized Multiple Negation According to the Function of Indefinite: By Social Class

The second observation concerns the two types of determiner tabulations, one including a as a potential multiple negative and the other excluding it. When a is excluded, approximately the same frequency of multiple negation is found for determiners and pronouns; when it is included, multiple negation is considerably less frequent for UMN and LWN speakers. How can the observed differences in frequency be explained?

Labov, et al. (1968: 280) have noted that the determiner a, which occurs (in both SE and NNE) with singular count nouns (e.g. a bird), should never be counted as a

potential multiple negative like the determiner any, which
occurs in negative sentences with plural count nouns (e.g.
any birds) and mass nouns (e.g. any people). That is, a
(e.g. He didn't have a bird) does not underlie no (e.g. He
didn't have no bird) in negative sentences. If Labov's
position is accepted, examples in which the determiner no
occurs with what is apparently a singular count noun must be
accounted for (e.g. I didn't have no pet (481:11); She didn't
want no bird to fly in (278:4)). By the same token, there
are also examples of a in negative sentences in which no does
NOT seem to be an alternant realization (i.e. it is ungrammatical in NNE), such as the following:

> If he ain't wanna teach he ain't gonna be a good
> teacher (406:75)
>
> but not:
>
> *If he ain't wanna teach he ain't gonna be no
> good teacher

> I can't remember a single prank (651:9)
>
> but not:
>
> *I can't remember no single prank

From these examples, it appears that, in some instances,
a can be counted as a potential multiple negative and in
others it cannot. The solution does NOT lie in a simple rejection of all instances of a in negative sentences as potential multiple negatives (the operational procedure which
Labov suggests). Rather, the relevant linguistic environments
in which a in negative sentences can be alternately realized
as no must be specified. The acceptability of no in the first
set of sentences (e.g. I didn't have no pet) and its unac-
ceptability in the second (e.g. *I can't remember no single
prank) can be accounted for by distinguishing between a
"generic" and "specific" function of the determiner. The

negative determiner no is an acceptable alternant of a when
the reference pertains to all members of a class (generic)
but unacceptable when the reference is restricted to a particular object or participant (specific). Although the
specific versus generic function of determiners has not consistently been maintained in traditional grammatical descriptions of English, Hale (1964) finds clear formal motivation
for this distinction.[12] For example, the indefinite determiner a functions generically in A Cadillac is always big,
but specifically in A Cadillac drove down the street and
parked by my house. The distinction between specific and
generic, both of which are realized as a in the singular,
is clearer in the plural where the forms are different; $\emptyset$
for generic (e.g. Cadillacs are big cars) and some for
specific (e.g. Some Cadillacs were parked by my house when
I came home).

On the basis of this distinction, we conclude that when
a functions generically, it may be realized as no in a negative sentence, and all examples of a in this context can be
tabulated as potential multiple negatives. When a functions
as a specific determiner, it may not be realized as a multiple
negative and therefore cannot be tabulated.[13]

5.2.3   Social Factors Intersecting with Social Class
5.2.3.1   Style

Although the reading passage contained several instances of
negative sentences occurring with indefinites (see Appendix
B), none of these was realized as a multiple negative. When
a potential multiple negative is read, the indefinite is read
in the form that appears in the text (e.g. I don't think any
of my friends ... is NOT read as I don't think none of my
friends ...).[14] An investigation of the frequency of multiple
negation in the first half of the interview as compared with

its frequency in the second half of the interview revealed
very little effect based on the different parts of the interview. Only in one instance, the LWN class, was there a difference of over 5 per cent (7.2 per cent) between the two
halves of the interview.

5.2.3.2 Sex

Fig. 45 presents the differences between the male and female
informants for the four Negro social classes.

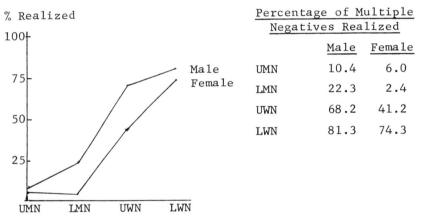

Fig. 45. Percentage of Realized Multiple Negation: By Social
          Class and Sex

Of the 7 working-class informants who show the categorical use of multiple negation, 5 are males and 2 are females.
On the other hand, of the 15 middle-class informants who indicate a qualitative absence of multiple negation, 9 are females
and only 6 are males.

5.2.3.3 Age

The factor of age as it intersects with social class is presented in Fig. 46.

    A consistently lower percentage of realized multiple
negation is found among the adult population. When the total

of 16 informants in each age group is combined for all social
classes, the adults (25.1 per cent) clearly contrast with the
pre-adolescents (49.1 per cent) and teen-agers (40.9 per cent).
Among the middle-class informants (UMN and LMN), only one adult
informant (a LMN male) has any realized multiple negation.   The
middle-class teen-agers (6.3 per cent) also reveal considerably
less multiple negation than the pre-adolescents (24.9 per cent).

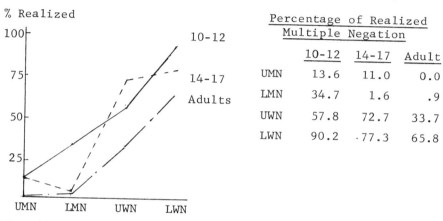

Fig. 46.   Percentage of Realized Multiple Negation: By Social
Class and Age

Among the working class, all adults show variation between realized and unrealized multiple negation; all seven
instances of the categorical operation of multiple negation
in the restricted counts are confined to teen-agers and pre-
adolescents.

5.2.3.4   Racial Isolation

The analysis of the UMN$_w$ informants reveals that there is a
qualitative absence of multiple negation. Of the UMN$_n$ informants, 4 of the informants reveal some (a mean of 14 per
cent) multiple negation. Two of these informants are pre-
adolescents and 2 teen-agers; no adults in the racially isolated group reveal multiple negation. Racial isolation is
therefore pertinent only to the pre-adolescents and teen-agers.

5.2.4 Summary

We have observed that several types of multiple negation occur among NNE speakers which do not typically occur among
nonstandard white speakers in Detroit (although they may
occur among Southern whites). These include: (1) the negativization of a pre-verbal auxiliary following a negative
indefinite (e.g. Nobody didn't do it); (2) negative inversion
of an indefinite and negativized auxiliary in declarative
sentences (e.g. Didn't nobody do it); and (3) transference of
negativized pre-verbal auxiliary outside the clause (e.g.
It wasn't no girls couldn't go with us).

Multiple negation reveals sharp social stratification.
In the majority of cases, the middle class (UMN and LMN) is
distinguished from the working class (UWN and LWN) by the
qualitative absence of multiple negation. On the other hand,
there are a few working-class speakers for whom the realization of multiple negation is categorical.

In a consideration of four different types of negative
constructions, multiple negatives involving negative adverbs
(e.g. didn't hardly; hardly never) show relatively less social
stigmatization than the other types of negative constructions.
The indefinite determiner a presents special problems in tabulating potential and realized multiple negation because there
are contexts (when it has a "specific" rather than a "generic"
function) in which a cannot be alternantly realized as no
(i.e. it is ungrammatical in NNE) in negative sentences.

The factors of sex and age are important as they intersect with social class to account for observed differences
in speech behavior. Racial isolation is a relevant factor
only as it is viewed in connection with age differences. Differences between the frequency of realized multiple negation
in the first and second half of the interview are not significant.

5.3 Copula/Auxiliary 'be' Absence

In a number of different syntactic environments the present
tense form of the copula or auxiliary[15] be is absent in the
speech of some Negroes. Copula absence is found in the following types of environments:

> Predicate Adjective

She real nice (278:10)

... he busy right now (565:8)

> Predicate Nominal

She a nurse (565:21)

They'll probably say that they the boss ... (489:64)

> Predicate Locative/Temporal

... they out there in space (369:8)

... he at Northwestern (583:11)

> Verb -ing

Do anything if you fighting (565:71)

If we fighting and we getting beat, I rather
one of my friends to jump in (583:20)

> Intentional Future 'gonna'

I really don't think John gonna make it (214:39)

Some say you gonna die (304:25)

In each of these environments copula absence may occur
when the construction is negative as well as positive (e.g.
He not German (369:35), ... they not a very good teacher
(208:29)).

Although there are a number of syntactic environments
where copula absence is found, there are also other environments in which copula PRESENCE regularly[16] occurs for NNE
speakers (Labov 1968: 5-8). The main environments in which
a copula regularly occurs are enumerated as follows:

(1) Environments in which the copula is in the past
     tense, e.g.:

Yesterday he was busy

(but not *Yesterday he busy)

(2) With first person singular forms, e.g.:

I'm a good man

(but not *I a good man)

(3) With non-finite (i.e. infinite, imperative, modal) be
constructions, e.g.:

He want to be good

(but not *He want to good)

(4) When the copula is in clause final position (as a result
of ellipsis, embedding, or inversion of some type), e.g.:

I know that's what they are

(but not *I know that's what they)

(5) In "tag" questions, e.g.:

He not home, is he?

(but not *He not home, he?)

(6) With existential emphasis, e.g.:

He is so bad! (as a response to the sentence 'He's
not bad')

(but not *He so bad)

(7) With the lexical items what's, that's, and it's
(phonetically in NNE [wəs], [ðæs], [ɪs]), e.g.:

(but not *I know that true)

The observation that there are syntactic environments in
which the copula is obligatorily realized in NNE is important
for several reasons. In the quantitative measurement of
copula absence, it is essential to separate environments
where there is no variability from those where there is legitimate variation between the presence and absence of the
copula. Failure to distinguish these environments would skew
the figures of systematic variation.

Another important consideration is the descriptive analysis of NNE. To ignore certain environments where the copula

is obligatorily realized in NNE can lead to an erroneous conclusion concerning the presence of an underlying (i.e. lexemic)
copula in a grammar of NNE.

A final reason is the relation that NNE copula absence
has to SE contraction (e.g. NNE He good = SE He's good).
Labov (1968: 9) suggests that "wherever SE can contract, NNE
can delete[17] is and are, and vice-versa; wherever SE cannot
contract, NNE cannot delete is and are, and vice versa."[18]
In all instances where the copula is obligatory in NNE, the
non-contracted form of the copula occurs in SE. For example,
in SE a contracted form cannot be used in clause-final position, so that a sentence such as *I know that's where they're
never occurs as an alternate of I know that's where they are.
Correspondingly, in NNE copula absence is not found in clause-
final position (e.g. *I know that's where they). Without
considering the environmental effect on copula variability,
this important correspondence is likely to be ignored.

5.3.1 Procedure for Tabulation

In the quantitative measurement, all instances in which is
and are forms of the copula might be realized are tabulated.
These environments involve predicate adjective, predicate
nominative, predicate locative, verb -ing, and intentional
future gonna. Not tabulated are environments in which the
copula is obligatorily realized, such as non-finite forms,
the items wha's, tha's and i's, copula in clause-final position, etc. (see sec. 5.3). Potential copula environments in
which the following word begins with a consonant or vowel
identical with the final segment of the contracted form
(e.g. he's silly) are also not counted since it is impossible
to perceive if the contracted form of the copula is actually
present or not.

Three categories of copula realization were codified:

(1) full copula forms (e.g. /ǰan iz biziy/ 'John is busy');
(2) contracted copula forms (e.g. /hiyz biziy/ 'he's busy');
and (3) complete absence of the copula (e.g. /hiy biziy/ 'he
busy'). The mean number of potential copulas was 25.5 per
informant.

5.3.2   The Correlation of Copula Absence with Social Class

In Fig. 47 the percentage of copula contraction and zero
realization are presented for the four Negro social groups
and the UMW (SE) group.[19]   For the UMW group, which does not
reveal any zero realization at all, the percentage of contracted forms is based only on the figures of 6 of the 12
informants in that group. The shaded area indicates the
percentage of zero realization and the clear area the percentage of contracted forms.

If the percentages of zero realization and contraction
are viewed independently, one notes that the working-class
informants (UWN and LWN) show a significantly higher frequency of zero realization and a significantly lower frequency of contraction. Viewing the totals of contraction
and zero realization together, an important relation between
contraction and zero realization is observed; namely, that
the combined percentages of contraction and zero realization
are approximately equivalent for all groups of speakers
(i.e. each of the groups has approximately the same frequency
of full forms). The social significance of this variable is
found in the different ratios of zero realization to contraction. This observation confirms Labov's observation that
NNE zero realization corresponds to SE contraction.

Labov (1968) has observed that there are several important constraints on the variability of contraction and
zero realization. He observes (1968: 16) that the single
most important constraint is whether the preceding phrase is

a pronoun (e.g. <u>He is good</u>) or a noun phrase (e.g. <u>The man</u>
<u>is good</u>). In Fig. 48 the figures are distinguished on the
basis of the preceding phrase. The shaded area indicates
the frequency of zero realization and the clear area the
frequency of contraction.

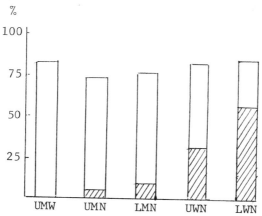

Percentage of Copula Contraction and Zero Realization

	Contraction		Zero Realization		
	Mean	Median	Mean	Median	Total (Mean)
UMW	79.8	86.4	0.0	0.0	79.8
UMN	67.9	73.7	4.7	3.7	72.6
LMN	63.3	66.7	10.9	10.0	74.2
UWN	40.1	42.2	37.3	34.1	77.4
LWN	25.0	21.4	56.9	58.9	81.9

Fig. 47. Percentage of Copula Contraction and Zero
Realization: By Social Class

The importance of the preceding phrase on the variability
of contraction and zero realization is observed in Fig. 48.
This constraint is quite regular for all groups. In the same
sense that a preceding pronoun effects greater contraction
in SE (see the UMW figures), it effects a significant increase
in zero realization among NNE speakers.

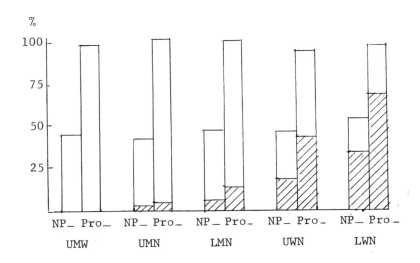

Percentage of Copula Contraction and Zero Realization

	Contraction		Zero Realization		Total	
	NP_	Pro_	NP_	Pro_	NP_	Pro_
UMW	45.6	96.2	0.0	0.0	45.6	96.2
UMN	39.3	92.2	1.8	6.2	40.8	98.4
LMN	40.0	83.1	6.3	13.8	46.3	96.9
UWN	24.3	49.4	18.9	40.7	43.2	90.1
LWN	20.5	32.4	30.1	63.1	50.6	95.5

Fig. 48. Percentage of Copula Contraction and Zero
Realization When Following a Noun Phrase
and Pronoun: By Social Class

On the basis of Fig. 48 one can predict that working-
class speakers will reveal the largest frequency of full
copula forms following noun phrases and the largest frequency of copula zero realization following pronouns. The
regularity with which this pattern is found for some speakers
is quite striking. Note, for example, the following passage:

Raymond, I think <u>he thirteen</u>. Oh, and I got another
one, he live back over that way -- <u>his name is Robert</u>.
I think <u>he eleven</u>. And I'm eleven and Lonnie Joe, <u>he
twelve</u> and <u>Little Man is fourteen</u> and <u>Richard is
twelve</u> (489:35).

Labov (1968: 16) has also observed that the following syntactical environment has some effect on the variability of copula contraction and zero realization. It is possible to distinguish five different types of following complement. They are, as mentioned previously (see sec. 5.3): predicate nominative (abbreviated PN); predicate adjective (abbreviated PA); predicate locative/temporal (abbreviated PL); verb -ing (abbreviated V-ing); and the intentional future gonna (abbreviated gn). Labov's analysis shows that there is a regular pattern of increase in the frequency of zero realization between these five types of complement, and that there is a corresponding increase in the frequency of contraction in SE based on these complement categories.

In Fig. 49 the effect of the following syntactical environment on contraction and zero realization is given. In order to insure that any figures for the following environments are simply not products of the variability of the preceding environment (i.e. pronouns or noun phrases) the tabulation is limited to environments in which the pronoun precedes the potential copula. In order to obtain sufficient numbers of examples for each of the five categories, the only class breakdown made is that between middle class (UMN and LMN) and working class (UWN and LWN).

The following syntactical environment does have some effect on the zero realization of the copula. The regularity of the increase between the different categories of complements confirms the pattern of increase noted by Labov (1968: 18) except in the case of predicate locatives. For this category, one can only conclude that zero realization is more frequent than predicate nominatives but less than intentional future gonna. The relative effect of predicate locative when compared with predicate adjective and verb -ing is inconclusive.

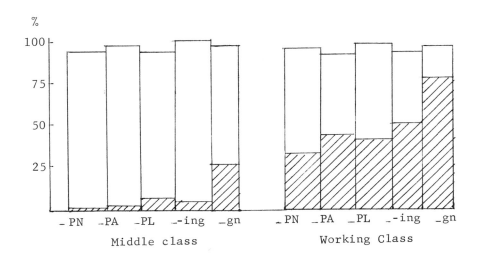

Percentage of Contraction and Zero Realization of Copula

	Contraction				
	_ PA	_ PN	_PL	_-ing	_gn
Middle Class	95.1	93.3	80.0	87.7	61.9
Working Class	55.7	42.1	53.6	39.3	3.3

	Zero Realization				
	_ PA	_PN	_PL	_-ing	_ gn
Middle Class	1.6	4.2	13.3	11.3	33.3
Working Class	36.5	47.3	44.4	50.0	78.9

Fig. 49. Percentage of Contraction and Zero Realization of
Copula When Preceded by a Pronoun and Followed by
a Predicate Adjective, Predicate Nominative,
Predicate Locative, Verb -ing, and gonna

The observations concerning the effect of the following
complement on zero realization has some important implications
in considering the social stigmatization of copula zero realization. The relatively high frequency with which zero realization is found preceding intentional future gonna among middle-
class informants suggests that zero realization preceding gonna

is less stigmatized than zero realization in other environments. Zero realization preceding gonna is found almost as
frequently among middle-class speakers as zero realization
preceding predicate nominatives is among working-class speakers.

Another important linguistic constraint on copula variability is whether the potential copula form is is (e.g. He
is busy) or are (e.g. They are busy). Since is sometimes
occurs with non-third person singular forms (e.g. They is
here), there are some cases for which it is difficult to
determine if the underlying form is is or are.[20] However,
since is actually is found to occur with non-third person
forms less than 5 per cent of the time, this small margin of
error will not greatly affect the observation of a regular
pattern. The percentages of contraction and zero realization
for is and are are given in Fig. 50.

An important effect on zero realization is observed in
Fig. 50. Although contraction plus zero realization is also
slightly higher for are than is, the difference is not nearly
as great as that between the percentage of zero realization
for the two forms. In most cases, the frequency of zero
realization of are is twice as great as the frequency for is.
There is only one working-class informant who does not have
some is contraction, but there are 7 of the 24 working-class
informants who have categorical absence of are contraction.

On the basis of Fig. 50 one can conclude that zero realization of is is considerably more socially stigmatized than
the zero realization of are. The zero realization of are for
each social class is greater than the zero realization of is
on the next lower social class. Thus, the UMN class has more
are zero realization than the LMN class has is zero realization; the LMN class more are zero realization than the UMW
class is zero realization; and the UWN class more are zero

realization than the LWN class is zero realization. One important reason for the predominance of are zero realization
over is can be attributed to the phonological pattern of
post-vocalic r absence (see sec. 4.4). The same type of
phonological pattern does not generally affect /s/ and /z/
absence.

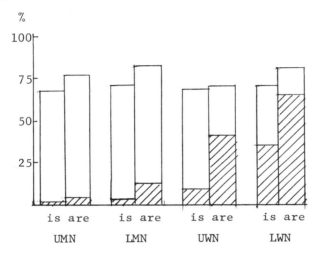

Percentage of Copula Contraction and Zero Realization

		IS			ARE	
	Contr.	Zero	Total	Contr.	Zero	Total
UMN	66.7	0.7	67.4	69.5	7.6	77.1
LMN	68.6	5.1	73.7	64.4	17.9	82.3
UWN	54.9	17.2	72.1	24.4	46.9	74.3
LWN	36.0	37.1	73.1	19.5	68.8	88.3

Fig. 50. Percentage of Contraction and Zero Realization
          of Copula When Underlying Form is IS and ARE:
          By Social Class

     Several issues can be raised concerning the function of
the copula in a NNE grammatical construct. One issue has been
whether or not an underlying (i.e. lexemic) copula can be
postulated for NNE.[21] For instance, Bailey (1965: 174,

1968: 574) has suggested that there is no underlying copula
as an integral part of the NNE grammatical system. Even if
one admits that some instances of copula presence result from
dialect importation, the evidence that there is an underlying
copula in NNE is clear. Formal motivation for this conclusion
is based on the fact that there are a number of environments
in which copula is categorically present for all NNE speakers,
including tag questions, copula in clause-final position, and
emphasis. The most economical analysis of NNE copula absence
(i.e. the one which allows the greatest generality in the
rules) is to consider it as a zero realization of an underlying copula in certain environments.

A less clear-cut issue concerning the function of copula
in NNE is the matter of copula contraction. Zero realization
of copula in NNE corresponds to contraction in SE and is the
predominant pattern for some working-class speakers. The
categorical absence of _are_ contraction for some speakers suggests that it is not an integral part of the NNE system for
them. The evidence for _is_ is not as strong, since the majority of speakers reveal considerable occurrence of contraction
as well as zero realization of _is_. If _is_ contraction is not
an integral part of NNE, this is true only for a small minority (probably children) of speakers.

A final issue concerning the zero realization of copula
is whether it should be considered as primarily a grammatical
or phonological pattern. Stewart (1966) and Bailey (1968)
consider the absence of the copula a grammatical pattern.
On the other hand, Labov (1968) treats it as a phonological
pattern. Labov considers zero copula realization as a phonological process (i.e. deletion) which operates on the /z/,
/s/,[22] or /r/ which remains after contraction has applied.
In the case of /r/, there is a corresponding phonological

pattern operating on post-vocalic lexical /r/ which reinforces
a phonological interpretation.[23]   In the case of /s/ and /z/
there is no parallel type of phonological pattern to re-
inforce a phonological interpretation. Labov maintains that
the absence of /s/ and /z/ is phonological because there is
a unique environment in which this phonological pattern is
applicable, namely, when /s/ or /z/ is preceded by an underlying word boundary.[24]   The crucial distinction between considering suffixal -Z on third person (see sec. 5.1.1) a
grammatical pattern and /s/ or /z/ copula a phonological pattern is that in the former case there is only a morpheme
boundary, whereas in the latter there is an underlying word
boundary.

Labov's interpretation can be rejected only if the
distinction between a morpheme and grammatical word boundary
is not recognized as a valid environment for phonological
conditioning. An additional, but less important reason for
rejecting Labov's interpretation is based on the observation
that the grammatical constraints on variability for this
variable are not typical of the types of constraints usually
found on phonological patterns. From Labov's viewpoint, any
lexical or grammatical factor can be appealed to as a valid
conditioning environment for phonological patterns as long
as they accountably represent the facts. The·question is how
much, if any, grammatical conditioning is allowed on phonological patterns. This question can hardly be answered within
the scope of this study, if in fact, it is answerable at all.
What one can conclude from this analysis is that both grammatical and phonological facts are necessary in order to give
an accountable description of the zero copula in NNE.

5.3.3 Social Factors Intersecting with Social Class
5.3.3.1 Style

In Fig. 51 the percentage of zero copula realization is presented for the three social groups contrasted in interview
and reading style. Only the figures for zero realization are
given.

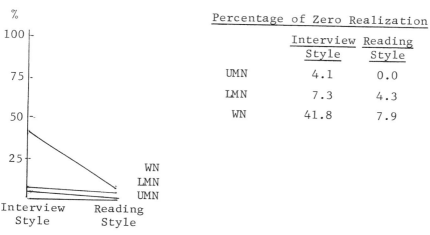

Percentage of Zero Realization

	Interview Style	Reading Style
UMN	4.1	0.0
LMN	7.3	4.3
WN	41.8	7.9

Fig. 51. Percentage of Copula Zero Realization: By Social
          Class and Style

Fig. 51 shows a sharp decrease in the frequency of zero
realization for the working-class informants. The variation
between the two styles parallels the variation found in the
other grammatical features much more than it does the stylistic variation of phonological features. For other grammatical
features, the working class showed significant stylistic shift
between the interview and reading styles but in the phonological variables there is generally slight variation between
interview and reading style.

5.3.3.2 Sex

In Fig. 52 the distribution of copula zero realization by sex
is given for the four Negro social groups.

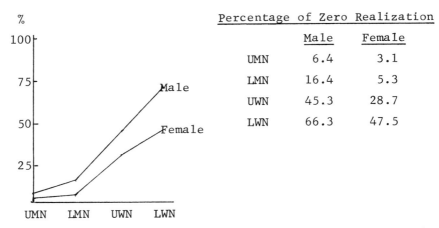

Fig. 52.   Percentage of Copula Zero Realization: By Social
Class and Sex

A consistent pattern of sex differentiation is observed
for all of the social classes in Fig. 52. Like other variables, the females reveal lower frequency of the socially
stigmatized variant than do the males.

5.3.3.3   Age

In Fig. 53 the percentage of zero realization is given for
the three age groups in each of the social classes.

The general pattern in Fig. 53 indicates that the adults
have less zero realization than both the pre-adolescents and
teen-agers. For the LMN and UWN classes, the incidence of
zero realization is considerably less for the teen-agers than
the pre-adolescents. Age distribution reveals the same type
of pattern than is found for other grammatical variables in
which the adults have less incidence of a stigmatized variant
than both pre-adolescents and teen-agers.

5.3.3.4   Racial Isolation

The UMN$_w$ shows 3.5 per cent and the UMN$_n$ shows 5.6 per cent
zero realization. The difference in the frequencies based
on the variable of racial isolation is thus minimal.

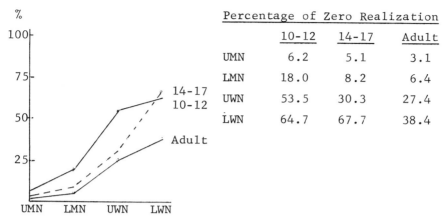

Percentage of Zero Realization			
	10-12	14-17	Adult
UMN	6.2	5.1	3.1
LMN	18.0	8.2	6.4
UWN	53.5	30.3	27.4
LWN	64.7	67.7	38.4

Fig. 53.   Percentage of Copula Zero Realization: By Social
           Class and Age

5.3.4   Summary

In the preceding discussion we have seen that copula zero
realization is an NNE feature which corresponds to contraction in SE. Several syntactical and phonological environments
affect the variability of copula zero realization, including
the preceding phrase, the following complement, and whether
the underlying form is _is_ or _are_.

In an NNE grammatical construct there is definitely an
underlying copula because of the number of environments in
which the copula is obligatorily realized. For some speakers
the contracted form of _are_ is entirely absent from their grammar, but the evidence for the contracted form of _is_ is not
nearly as clear. The question of whether copula zero realization is basically a phonological or grammatical pattern is
dependent on the extent to which one allows grammatical conditioning of phonological patterns. In this analysis it has
simply been suggested that both phonological and grammatical
facts are necessary to give an accountable description of
NNE zero copula.

The factors of style, sex, and age all intersect with social class in accounting for variation, but racial isolation is of minimal importance.

5.4 Invariant 'be'

In addition to the absence of the copula in NNE (see sec. 5.3) the "unconjugated", or "invariant"[25] form of be is found where the present tense, conjugated forms of the verb be (i.e. am, are, is) occur in SE. It occurs in many of the same types of syntactical environments as the conjugated, finite forms of the copula and auxiliary in SE as indicated in the following examples.

Predicate Nominal

He sometimes be a operator doctor (487:36)

Whoever tags the person that's calling "red light" or "green light" you be the, you know, the person up there (304:9)

Predicate Adjective

They sometimes be incomplete and things like that (487:24)

Sometime when they do it, most of the problems always be wrong (521:15)

Predicate Locative/Temporal

Well, it mostly be in the evening when they play hide-and-go-seek (305:3)

That's why I wonder why I don't see him -- he usually be 'round (583:5)

Verb -ing

On Hallowe'en put a knife or fork or something under your bed 'cause the, a witch be riding around (489:57)

Well, sometime she be fighting in school and out on the playground (444:29)

Invariant be has recently attracted considerable attention from linguists because it appears to have a grammatical

function which is distinct to the NNE verbal system. William
A. Stewart (1965), who first suggested that be marked a grammatical category of "habitual" or "durative" in NNE, observes
that there is no equivalent grammatical category in SE. Before considering the social stratification of invariant be,
it will be necessary to describe its grammatical function and
evaluate the various descriptive analyses of it.

To define the grammatical function of be the contexts in
which it occurs must be analyzed. Crystal (1966) has pointed
out that one of the most important clues to the verb tense
categories in English is found in adverb co-occurrence restrictions. Particularly important are what Crystal (1966:
11) calls the "frequency of occurrence" adverbs, which refer
to how often a particular event or state takes place. These
types of adverbs co-occur with be quite regularly. Of the
184 examples of be found in this corpus, 48 co-occur with an
adverb indicating the repeated occurrence of an activity,
such as sometimes, usually, and every time. Crystal (1966:
11) maintains that there are several subcategories of adverbs
referring to the repeated or continuous occurrence of an
activity. In Table 14 the number of be examples co-occurring
with each adverb subcategory is given for all working-class
speakers who have some incidence of invariant be. In addition to the number of be examples with each adverb type, the
total number of each adverb type and the percentage of each
adverb with be is given.

The percentages of adverb subtype with be are quite
close, although the actual number of adverbs with be is
considerably higher for occasional and usual occurrence adverb types. In addition to the occurrence of be with these
adverb subtypes, 17 examples of be occur with when (e.g.
When you be 'it', you have to hide your eyes and hunt for
'em (278:1)). In all of these examples, when refers to an

Table 14

Types of Adverbs Co-occurring With Invariant _Be_

Adverb Subtype	Examples	No. with 'be'	Total No.[26] Adv. Occ.	% with 'be'
Rare Occ.	hardly, very seldom	4	31	12.9
Occasional Occ.	sometimes, some days	22	135	16.3
Usual Occ.[27]	usually, mostly	16	120	13.3
Continuous Occ.	always, all the time	4	35	11.4

indefinite event which may take place at various intervals
(i.e. _whenever_). If these 17 examples (out of a total of 62
sentences in which _when_ with this meaning occurs) are classified with the adverbs of occasional occurrence, there are 39
incidences of _be_ with this adverb type (19.8 per cent of the
total number of occasional adverbs found in the texts). The
relatively ·high numbers of examples of _be_ with occasional and
usual adverbs causes Fasold (forthcoming) to suggest that the
meaning of _be_ may be defined as follows:

> The meaning of '_be_' involves predication which happens
> repeatedly, but not continuously. At any moment the
> predication may be valid, but there are gaps between
> instances of the event described.

Although one might infer that _be_ may NOT be used in any
context referring to a single specific occurrence of an event
or state, there are some examples in which _be_ seems to refer
to a single occurrence of an activity, such as the following
sentences:

I _be_ 12 February 7 (uttered the preceding July)
(461:41)

<u>He be in in a few minutes</u> (spoken several minutes
prior to the entrance of the subject) (447:4)

<u>I been working there since 'bout January ...
coupla more weeks it be six months</u> (304:18)

In these examples the event or state refers to a single
non-repeated state of activity which will take place at some
specific time in the future. How can these sentences be
accounted for if one defines the function of <u>be</u> only with
reference to a non-continuous repeated activity or state?
We must either abandon our previous definition of <u>be</u> or consider the above examples to be the realization of an underlying source different from <u>be</u> which refers to an intermittent activity or state. It has already been observed
that the illustrations of <u>be</u> referring to a single occurrence
of an event are found in a future context. Can <u>be</u> refer to
a single occurrence of an event only if it is in a future
context? If so, what is peculiar about the future context
which explains this usage? One solution is to view the use
of <u>be</u> in a future context as the realization of an underlying <u>will be</u>[28] and in non-future contexts as the realization
of <u>be</u> marking an intermittent activity or state. This suggestion is supported by evidence from constructions where an
auxiliary is obligatorily realized in NNE. The most diagnostic types of constructions for determining the underlying
auxiliary are negatives, "tag" questions, and elliptical verb
phrases. If <u>be</u> in a sentence such as <u>He be in in a few
minutes</u> is the realization of <u>will be</u> one can expect the
negative form of the sentence to be:

<u>He won't be in in a few minutes</u>.

the tag question to be:

<u>He be in in a few minutes, won't he</u>?

and the elliptical verb phrase to be:

<u>He be in in a few minutes, I know he will</u>.

Fasold,[29] in a test constructed specifically to elicit the types of auxiliaries used with be, has substantially documented that these constructions regularly occur for the negative, tag question, and elliptical verb phrase. These contrast with the formation of the negative, tag, and elliptical verb phrase for be when it marks an intermittent activity in a sentence such as Sometimes he be busy.

> Sometime he don't be busy.
>
> Sometime he be busy, don't he?
>
> Sometime he be busy, I know he do.

The fact that be referring to a future activity takes the auxiliary will, and be referring to an intermittent activity takes do as an auxiliary indicates the different underlying sources of be. Labov, et al. (1968: 239) observe that the be of will be is the result of a phonological pattern which operates on the contracted form of will be (i.e. will be → 'll be → be). The absence (or vocalization) of post-vocalic laterals in lexical items of NNE speakers (e.g. school, boil, etc.) is cited (Labov, et al. 1968: 238) as reinforcing evidence that be derived from will be is the result of a phonological pattern.

In addition to some instances of be which have an underlying will, some examples are realizations of the past tense form of the will auxiliary, would.[30] The negative, tag question, and elliptical verb phrase formations of a sentence such as If he got a walkie-talkie, he be happy provide evidence for this conclusion. On the basis of Fasold's elicitation test, the negative is:

> If he didn't get a walkie-talkie, he wouldn't be happy.

the tag question:

> If he got a walkie-talkie, he be happy, wouldn't he?

and the elliptical verb phrase:

> If he got a walkie-talkie, he be happy, I know he would.

In the same sense that be with an underlying will can be
viewed as a phonological pattern operating on the contracted
form of the auxiliary, it is also possible to view be which
is the realization of would be as a phonological pattern
operating on the contracted form 'd be. In the discussion
of the phonological variables we observed that zero realization of the phoneme d in syllable-final position sometimes
occurs in NNE (see sec. 4.3). The phonological solution of
be with underlying would is thus based on a phonological pattern far more general than this single item.

The evidence for three underlying sources of be is not
limited to elicited constructions. A number of examples
taken from conversations also suggest that be is the realization of different sources. For example, the context of the
following utterances suggests an underlying will:

> By the time I grow up, you know, a lotta things
> change and it be different opportunities for jobs
> and different times will be here (726:8)

> I think I'll just stay at home and if the service
> want me come and get me -- I be right here at home for
> quite some time (214:36)

Similarly, there are contexts which suggest an underlying
would:

> I used to day-dream, I used to drift off in my own
> little world, and she just be talking and I wouldn't
> listen to a word she was saying (278:6)

> Well, I used to hang around with this Puerto Rican
> girl ... She be talking and you couldn't understand a
> thing she be saying... (278:10)

There are also a number of cases of be with the negative
auxiliary don't which suggests that NO underlying will or
would is present:

> They don't be mean (565:41)

> See, we pass from class to class, we don't be in the
> same one (526:8)

Although many instances of be suggest the particular
underlying source for be from the surrounding context, there
are also examples for which there is inadequate context to
determine the underlying source. Given the sentence He be
home, it is possible to interpret it in one of three ways.
In the context He be home in a few minutes, it would normally
be understood to have an underlying will; in the context If
he didn't have to go away he be home, it would normally be
understood to have an underlying would; in the context Sometimes he be at home and sometime he don't, it would normally
be understood as be referring to an intermittent activity or
state.

An adequate understanding of the function of be in NNE
is dependent on distinguishing between its three underlying
sources. Be with underlying will or would is used similarly
to the way will be and would be are used in SE, but be which
marks intermittent activity or state is used in NNE in a way
which is not equivalent to any SE construction. Although
present tense (or technically more correct, non-past tense)
use of the copula in SE sometimes includes the notion of
habituality, it is essential not to equate the two. For
example, present tense in SE may co-occur with adverbs referring to a single specific occurrence as well as a repeated
activity. Thus, the sentences He's busy right now and Sometimes he's busy are both grammatical in SE. In my corpus,
be co-occurring with an adverb of single occurrence in a
present tense context is conspicuously absent. On the basis
of this significant absence it can be inferred that a sentence
such as *He be busy right now is ungrammatical in NNE. Unfortunately, the responses of working-class speakers to
linguistic grammaticality in NNE are highly suspect, since
the informant's reason for rejecting a sentence may not be
based on linguistic grammaticality. However, the several

instances in which NNE speakers have responded to this sentence, they judged it as an unacceptable NNE sentence. On
the other hand, the NNE sentence He busy right now, which is
unmarked for intermittent activity in NNE, was accepted as a
grammatical NNE sentence by these speakers.

Another reason for maintaining that the use of be in NNE
is not a simple correspondence of present tense in the SE
copula is that be cannot refer to a permanent continuous
relationship. Reference to a continuing permanent relationship in a sentence such as *He be my father is ungrammatical.[31]
The grammatical form of this sentence in NNE is He my father.
In SE the present tense form of the copula is used to refer
to a continuous relationship (e.g. He is my brother). One
can only conclude that this NNE category has no isomorphic
correspondence in SE. Various labels have been attached to
this category, including such terms as "habitual", "iterative",
"durative", "general", etc. Although the predications are
usually distributed over points in time (e.g. sometimes he be
here), Fasold notes that occasionally it is the subject and
not the predicate which shows the distribution:

> In the sentence "Every time I get in a fight, they
> be smaller than me", it is not that the predication
> "be smaller" is true of the same persons at differ-
> ent points in time, but that at different times there
> will be various people, all of whom are smaller than
> the speaker. Similarly, when one boy was asked what
> a stingray looked like, he replied, "Some of them be
> big and some of them be small". Certainly any par-
> ticular bicycle is permanently either big or small,
> but at different points of time, one might encounter
> bicycles and at any time one of these may be either
> small or big (Fasold forthcoming).

Because the reference occasionally affects subjects as
well as predicates, this feature is termed "distributive"
instead of using a label (e.g. "habitual", "iterative") which
has exclusive reference to predication. Much more essential

than the terminological label is the function of 'distributive be' -- an activity or state which takes place at various
non-continuous intervals.

Having suggested a descriptive analysis of be which accounts for the examples in my corpus, the various analyses
of invariant be which have been proposed recently can be re-
viewed. These include the views of Loflin (forthcoming),
Feigenbaum (forthcoming), Labov, et al. (1968), and Fasold
(forthcoming).[32]

Loflin (forthcoming) considers be to be a marker of
what he calls "a-temporal tense" in NNE. He treats it as a
category mutually exclusive with present, definite past, and
indefinite past tense in NNE. Concerning the label "a-
temporal", Loflin (forthcoming) notes:

> ... it [the term a-temporal] is the result of the
> observation that be co-occurs with time adverbs and
> in discourse contexts which are neither future, pre-
> sent, nor past but potentially any of these depending
> upon the structural context. The following sentences
> are examples of this kind:
>
> (48) a. They be here tomorrow
>   b. They be here all the time
>   c. They be dancing with each other   (In this
>   last example, the context implied past
>   time; the informant said he went to a
>   party where he sat out the dances in a
>   corner; I asked him what the other people
>   did there. Whereupon he replied with
>   (48c).

In Loflin's analysis, all occurrences of invariant be
are realizations of the same underlying source. Sentences
such as They be here tomorrow and They be here all the time
are treated as realizations of the same underlying source
even though, in the former case, the reference may be to the
single occurrence of an event in the future and in the latter
case it may not. Loflin admits that the sentence They be here
tomorrow might be considered a matter of "will reduction" but

dismisses this possibility because will reduction cannot
apply for sentences (48b) and (48c). His rejection of an
underlying will for (48a) on the basis of "the non-generaliz-
ability of will reduction" is inconsistent with the facts
concerning negative and elliptical verb phrase formations.
In essence, his rejection is based on his failure to recognize neutralization. Neutralization, the relationship in
which one lower level unit can be the realization of two or
more underlying units, is a well-known and common phenomenon
in language and one must ask why it may not be expected in
the case of be.

   Before leaving Loflin's notion of a-temporality, his
observation that be may occur in past tense contexts such as
sentence (48c) must also be considered. Occurrences of be
in past tense contexts are quite rare so that we must look
closely at the examples we find in order to make sure that
we have an unambiguously past tense context. In this corpus
there are no occurrences of be in an unambiguously past tense
context. The context of Loflin's example can hardly be considered unambiguous. We may ask if the fieldworker's question,
occurring in the past tense, could actually have been answered
in a non-past context (a not uncommon occurrence in an interview situation). That is, the informant may actually have
been referring to the fact that people habitually dance at
parties while he sits in the corner watching. Or, the informant could have been describing an event or series of
events in the past in a way similar to how SE speakers use
the "historical present". That is, a non-past context is
used for an event or series of events which have already taken
place. At any rate, the example on which Loflin bases his
argument for the occurrence of be in a past context cannot
be considered a dianostic sentence for the use of be is an
unambiguous past context. A diagnostic sentence for the

past context of be might be:

> Last year sometime he be at the playground and
> sometime he didn't

If Loflin's position is accepted, one has to admit that be
can co-occur with past tense adverbs such as last year and
that the past tense of the pro-verb did may refer to be.
Neither of these types of co-occurrences has been found in
my corpus.[33]

Like Loflin, Feigenbaum's (forthcoming) analysis does
not distinguish be which is the realization of will be, or
would be from be which has no underlying will or would.
The evidence from elliptical verb phrases and negative formations certainly suggests that any analysis which fails to
recognize the different underlying sources realized in be is
inadequate. Furthermore, any view which must reconcile the
use of be in the future, where it may refer to a single occurrence of an event, with its non-future usage, where it
refers only to an event or state which occurs intermittently,
must be held in suspicion.

Feigenbaum rejects any analysis which describes the
distinctive feature of the be construction as one in which
an event or state is repeated intermittently. He suggests
that be is a marker of "temporary, limited continuity".
At first glance, it may appear that his disagreement is more
terminological than analytical and that the label "temporary,
limited continuity" is essentially not much different from
the designation of some uses of be as "distributive",
"habitual", or "iterative". A closer look at Feigenbaum's
position reveals that he objects to any description of be
as an event or state which occurs intermittently, whatever
terminological label it may carry. He asks:

> The construction be selling has been called "habitual"
> or "repetitive" but is this a grammatical opposition
> which serves to differentiate two constructions or is

it a description of one characteristic use of this
construction? (Feigenbaum forthcoming)

Feigenbaum then suggests:

It is not the grammatical construction itself that
conveys the sense of "habitual", "repetitive" etc.;
it is the time indication, either in the adverbial
modification used or in the context of the conversation
(Feigenbaum forthcoming).

Because of the overwhelming number of cases in which
'distributive be' co-occurs with habitual or distributive
type adverbs and the numerous instances in which it occurs
in discourse contexts where events are repeated at various
intervals, the question then becomes: are there any contexts
in which be unambiguously does NOT have reference to a re-
curring event but DOES have reference to an activity "continuing temporarily". Feigenbaum suggests that there is
such a context and offers the following illustration:

I once asked a teen-age boy whether he would accept
[the sentence] Francis pool be open. He did not accept
it, but of course (as I discovered later), this was to
be expected. The question was asked on July 1 -- in
the middle of the summer -- at which time the state
was not viewed as continuing temporarily but as repeated
(Feigenbaum forthcoming).

We have already suggested that tests of acceptability
concerning NNE are somewhat suspicious because of the social
status NNE occupies. Assuming, however, that the informant
did respond purely to the question of linguistic grammaticality, the example is still not conclusive. Without any
co-occurring adverbs or clear-cut discourse context setting
up a diagnostic linguistic context there is no way of knowing
that the informant was responding to the question as was intended. For example, how do we know that the question was
not understood to refer to whether the pool was open at the
particular moment the question was asked (e.g. Francis pool
be open right now), in which case the sentence would be

rejected because it referred to an immediate rather than a
repeated event. Or, the informant might have rejected it
because he viewed the opening of the pool as one continuous
event which conceptually covered the span of the summer (as
opposed to the winter, during which it was closed), not as
an event which occurred daily. That is, the informant's con-
ception of the event may have been different from the real
life occurrence of the pool opening and closing daily. However the informant may have interpreted the sentence, this
isolated case cannot be considered as a definitive counter-
example to the view that repeated activity is the distinctive
feature of be without a clear-cut linguistically diagnostic
context. If no unambiguous context can be delimited in which
the feature of "intermittent activity or state" cannot fit
all instances of 'distributive be', the labeling of be is
reduced to a terminological debate.

The view of Labov, et al. (1968) differs from Loflin's
and Feigenbaum's in that they recognize that be may be derived from different underlying sources. In their analysis,
be which is the realization of will be is distinguished from
be which has no underlying will. No mention of be derived
from would be is found in Labov's description so that one can
only speculate whether he admits be to be the realization of
would be as well as will be. As we shall see later, there is
some indication that Labov has overlooked be as the realization of would be.

Rather than give one distinctive component which is
common to all uses of non-future be, Labov, et al. suggest
that there are several components which usually coincide.
Among the most common ones are "general" ("general conditions
extending over a period of time, usually indefinite in force"
(Labov, et al. 1968: 231)), "iterative" ("where an event occurs
habitually" (Labov, et al. 1968: 231)), and "indefinite"

("an indefinite durative sense, or more precisely, a state
of affairs" (Labov, et al. 1968: 232)). Labov, et al. suggest
(1968: 232) that "those who would search for a conjunctive
definition might try to specify 'non-temporal' or 'non-
finite', which may or may not be equivalent to 'indefinite'."
The description of be as indicating a general, habitual, or
indefinite state of affairs does not conflict with the view
that the feature marking non-future be is 'distributive'.
However, it is also suggested that there are uses of be in
a non-future context which may refer to "an instant state of
affairs"; this use is considered ungrammatical NNE in the
analysis suggested here. Labov, et al. (1968: 232) state:

> Furthermore, we find two clear examples of be₂ [i.e.
> the non-conjugated form of be] used to describe an
> 'instant state' of affairs:
>
> (185) We shake hands. And that be₂ it. (36, Ala, #883)
>
> (186) The last guy who be₂ picked, they IT. (11, T-Birds,
>   #498)
>
> Although there is no adverb here to define the semantics
> of the situation, it seems clear to us that in (185)
> that be₂ it at that moment and (for a well defined
> period thereafter) [sic]. (186) seems an even clearer
> representation of the instant state which comes into
> being at that moment: when the guy is picked, he becomes
> at that moment, IT. Neither the first or second clauses
> can be described as a-temporal.
>
> Finally, we find one very clear case of the adjoining be
> with an adverb of instantaneous time.
>
> (187) If he hit me--...
>   He probably just hit me, 'cause he be mad
>   right then; you know he wouldn't hit me
>   otherwise. (15, Oscar Brothers, #584)
>
> It seems clear to us that no twists or turns or meta-
> phorical interpretations can escape the implications
> of this last example.

Although Labov, et al. insist that these examples can
only be viewed as the use of be referring to an instant state
of affairs, both (185) and (186) can be viewed as a state
which occurs at different intervals. For example, in (186),
whenever one plays tag, an activity which occurs at various
intervals in a child's experience, the child who is tagged
last is 'it'. Sentences like this are quite common and seem
to be one of the characteristic ways in which 'distributive
be' is used.

Despite the strong warning that (187) can only be considered a counter-example of the view that 'distributive be'
occurs only with repeated types of events, a closer view of
this example must be taken. What Labov fails to see is that
the use of be in this construction is apparently derived from
underlying would be (e.g. an alternate realization might be:
He'd probably just hit me 'cause he'd be mad right then; you
know he wouldn't hit me otherwise). The fact that wouldn't
is used in the following clause certainly suggests that be
in this case can be derived from would be. We have already
observed that be which has underlying will or would must be
considered quite different from 'distributive be'; one of the
main reasons for this difference is the fact that this use
may refer to a single occurrence of an event or state. The
oversight of Labov, et al. seems to stem from their failure
to recognize the underlying would in this example. We thus
conclude that Labov, et al. offer no clear-cut counter-examples
demonstrating that 'distributive be' refers to a single occurrence of an event or state.

Finally, we turn to Fasold's treatment of be (forthcoming).
Fasold recognizes the important difference between be with an
underlying will or would and other instances of be which refer
to an event which occurs at various intervals in time. He
maintains that the feature which is common to all occurrences

of 'distributive be' is the non-continuous repeated occurrence
of an activity. In this sense, there is essentially no difference in the analysis of the distinctive component of be
in Fasold's description and the one presented on the basis
of my corpus. The major difference between the two views
is the way in which this feature is represented in the grammar of NNE. Instead of treating be as a distinct grammatical
category such as 'distributive', 'habitual', or 'iterative',
Fasold suggests that 'distributive be' is most adequately
represented as the absence of the category "tense". That is,
for the NNE copula the choice of tense is optional. If tense
is not chosen, then the form be with a distributive or iterative meaning is realized; if tense is chosen, then the regular choices between certain categories of tense (past tense
versus non-past) are applicable. In the grammar of NNE,
tense is optional only for be; other finite verb forms are
always marked for tense. The restriction of "tenselessness"
to be raises several questions about the use of the pro-verb
do when be is its antecedent. In a sentence such as He
usually be busy, I know he do, be is presumably tenseless,
but what is the status of do with respect to tense? If do
is also considered tenseless, then tenselessness is not as
restricted as Fasold suggests. On the other hand, if do is
a present tense pro-verb then Fasold must explain how a
present tense pro-verb can have a tenseless form as its antecedent.

Another crucial consideration in Fasold's description
is the assumption that be may never occur in a past tense
context. This means that the sentence Last year, sometime
he be at the playground and sometime he didn't must be considered ungrammatical in NNE. If one admits that the past
tense form of the pro-verb did may have be as its antecedent
he would have to admit that tense and distributive may

co-occur. If these co-occur, then distributive be cannot be
considered simply as a function of the absence of the formal
grammatical category tense. We have already observed that if
examples of 'distributive be' and past tense do co-occur they
are quite rare. In the analysis proposed in this study it is
possible that these may co-occur without being forced to
abandon the formal analysis. Fasold would be forced to seriously alter his formal representation of be in the NNE grammar if this were the case.

5.4.1   Procedure for Tabulation

In previous descriptions of linguistic variables, quantitative
measurement has been done on the basis of actual and potential realizations of particular variants of a variable. Invariant be presents special problems if this same method is
adopted. One could conceivably count all present tense forms
of conjugated be (i.e. am, is, are) and consider the relative
frequency of invariant be on the basis of the number of invariant be forms in relation to the number of conjugated forms.
This is how Labov, et al. (1968: 236) have tabulated the relative frequency of invariant be. This measurement seems inadequate for several reasons. In the first place, there are
examples of invariant be which may NOT simply substitute for
all incidences of conjugated be forms. 'Distributive be'
cannot occur where the conjugated forms of be refers to a
single occurrence of an event or to a continuous permanent
relationship. Therefore a tabulation of conjugated forms of
be in relation to invariant be is an inadequate representation
of its actual frequency. Another reason is the fact that be
with underlying will and would cannot be considered as alter-
nating with conjugated be forms. An adequate tabulation of
be with underlying will or would (e.g. He be here tomorrow)
has to include all incidences in which will be or would be

occur as potential cases of future be (e.g. He will be here
tomorrow). A final reason is that invariant be in be verb
-ing constructions might be considered to alternate with non-
verb -ing forms in some instances (e.g. Sometimes he be doing
his work and Sometimes he do his work). The exact types of
contexts in which a form such as he do is considered a potential occurrence of he be doing are not clear, since a careful
analysis of the so-called present tense in NNE has not been
carried out as a part of this analysis. The exact relationship of a construction such as he be doing to he do in NNE
must precede any quantitative measurement depending on the
principle of potential versus actual presence of invariant
be.

This variable has been tabulated by simply counting the
number of invariant be incidences for the entire interview.[34]
Although this quantitative method is less preferred than the
tabulation of potential and actual occurrences of invariant
be, we shall observe that it is still adequate for revealing
the social distribution of this variable.

5.4.2 The Correlation of Invariant 'Be' with Social Class

In Fig. 54 the mean and median number of occurrences of invariant be per informant are given for the four social classes
of Negroes. No figures are given for the UMW informants since
invariant be is categorically absent for this group.

The occurrence of invariant be among middle-class speakers is quite rare. Only 5 of 24 middle-class informants (UMN
and LMN) have any occurrences of invariant be at all. Among
UWN speakers the mean number of occurrences of invariant be
per informant is only 3. But among LWN informants there are
approximately 11 occurrences per informant. Most of the
other variables have not shown a great amount of difference

between the UWN and LWN class, but for this variable there is
a significant difference between the two working-class groups.

Number of Occurrences Per Informant	Average Number of Occurrences of Invariant 'be' Per Informant	
	Mean	Median
UMN	0.4	0.0
LMN	0.5	0.0
UWN	3.5	3.0
LWN	10.9	10.0

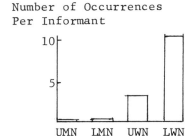

Fig. 54.   Average Number (Mean and Median) of Occurrences
           of Invariant be Per Informant: By Social Class

Invariant be can also be tabulated according to its different uses. All occurrences of be can be divided on the
basis of four categories: (1) those where the context indicates it is used in a 'distributive' sense; (2) those which
are derived from underlying will be; (3) those which are
derived from underlying would be; and (4) those where the
underlying source is ambiguous (e.g. it may be the realization of underlying will be or 'distributive be'). The distribution of be in terms of these four categories is given in
Table 15.

Table 15

Distribution of the Uses of Invariant Be

	'distributive be' No. of Ex.	will be No. of Ex.	would be No. of Ex.	ambiguous No. of Ex.
UMN	2	2	--	1
LMN	2	--	--	4
UWN	21	3	5	14
LWN	69	8	7	47

The most frequent use is 'distributive be'. There are many examples which remain ambiguous despite the fact that the role of context in "disambiguating" be was considered in the tabulation. The large number of ambiguous cases involve be which may be the realization of underlying will be or 'distributive be'. The ambiguity between these two items is due to the fact that the modal will sometimes has an habitual or iterative force, a meaning which is quite close to the meaning of 'distributive be'.[35] For example, in an SE sentence such as Whenever he is around his friends he'll be bad, but when he's around us, he'll be good, will is used in a context referring to an habitual event. This same type of habitual use of will has also been observed among NNE speakers. This means that when we encounter a sentence such as When he be around his friends, he mess around, it is possible to view be as the realization of underlying 'distributive be'. This type of overlap between the meaning of will be and 'distributive be' accounts for practically all examples of ambiguity.

Although other types of quantitative measurement could be made to investigate the effect of independent linguistic variables on the relative frequency of invariant be (e.g. surrounding syntactical environments), this has not been attempted here. Without considering the actual realization of be in relation to its potential occurrences, it cannot be determined if the differences revealed in such tabulations would be attributable to the greater potential occurrences of invariant be in particular types of syntactical environments or whether they would reveal actual systematic variation.

5.4.3 Social Factors Intersecting with Social Class
5.4.3.1 Style

On the basis of the distinction between interview and reading

style, it can only be observed that no instances of invariant
be occur in the reading passages. Within the interview itself,
no formal distinction between different styles was made.
Because of the distinct function of 'distributive be', however, the occurrence of invariant be is found in certain
types of discourse genre much more than in others. Descriptions of games, customary activities during holidays, and
the description of usual activities in work or school reveal
many more occurrences of be than the narration of particular
television programs or movies.

5.4.3.2 Sex

In Fig. 55 the distribution of be according to sex and social
class is presented.

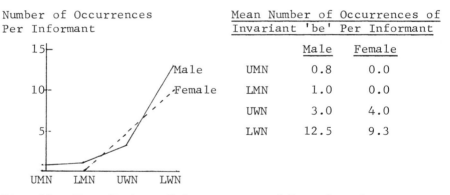

Number of Occurrences Per Informant	Mean Number of Occurrences of Invariant 'be' Per Informant		
		Male	Female
	UMN	0.8	0.0
	LMN	1.0	0.0
	UWN	3.0	4.0
	LWN	12.5	9.3

Fig. 55.   Mean Number of Occurrences of Invariant be
           per Informant: By Social Class and Sex

There is a slight difference in the overall number of
occurrences of invariant be based on sex, although for the
UWN class the females have more occurrences of be than the
males. The general pattern confirms the conclusions of previously discussed variables, namely, that females use stigmatized linguistic variants less frequently than males.

5.4.3.3 Age

The distribution of invariant be by age and social class is
presented in Fig. 56.

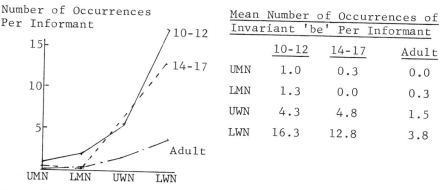

Number of Occurrences
Per Informant

Mean Number of Occurrences of
Invariant 'be' Per Informant

	10-12	14-17	Adult
UMN	1.0	0.3	0.0
LMN	1.3	0.0	0.3
UWN	4.3	4.8	1.5
LWN	16.3	12.8	3.8

Fig. 56. Mean Number of Occurrences of Invariant be
          per Informant: By Social Class and Age

There are important age differences in the frequency of
invariant be based on age. Invariant be is a feature characteristic of working-class pre-adolescent and teen-age speech.
This variable is one of the most marked features for age differentiation among the working-class informants.

5.4.3.4 Racial Isolation

None of the UMN_w have any incidence of invariant be. Of the
UMN_n informants, two of the informants, one pre-adolescent and
one teen-ager, use invariant be. Between these two speakers,
there are only five occurrences of invariant be. Although the
factor of racial isolation may help explain the usage of be by
these two informants, on the whole, racial isolation is not of
great importance in viewing this feature for UMN informants.

5.4.4 Summary

In the analysis of invariant be we have seen that be may be
the realization of three different sources: (1) 'distributive

be', a grammatical category marking the repeated non-continuous
occurrence of an activity of state; (2) the modal will plus be;
and (3) the past tense form of will (i.e. would) plus be.
When will be or would be is the underlying source, be functions
in a way quite similar to the corresponding SE modals. 'Distributive be' marks a category which is unique to the NNE grammatical system. In addition to co-occurrence restrictions which
indicate these three underlying sources for be, the formation
of negatives, tag questions, and elliptical verb phrases clearly
reveal the different underlying sources of be.

There is a three-way stratification of the social groups
on the basis of be -- between the middle class (UMN and LMN)
and between the UWN and LWN classes. Sex and age are important
factors intersecting with social class to account for observed
differences in the incidence of be.

5.5   The Sociolinguistic Function of the Grammatical Variable:
Conclusion

Having described the sociolinguistic function of the grammatical variables independently, we now turn to some general
conclusions concerning the nature of the grammatical variable.
Two main areas are discussed: (1) the social function of the
grammatical variable; and (2) the linguistic function of the
grammatical variable.

5.5.1   The Social Function of the Grammatical Variable

Several questions can be raised on the basis of the independent discussion of grammatical variables. As we did with the
phonological variables (see sec. 4.5.1), we can ask if the
grammatical differences between the different social groups
are mainly quantitative or qualitative. Are particular social
groups characterized by the categorical absence or presence of
particular variants, or are the groups simply differentiated

by the frequency with which certain variants occur? The grammatical variables considered here reveal that the middle class
(UMN and LMN) is characterized by the categorical absence of
particular variants. The clear majority of middle-class informants indicate that certain stigmatized variants are categorically absent. This does not mean that in restricted subcategories of a variable the differences are qualitative
rather than quantitative. For example, multiple negatives
involving a negativized auxiliary and an inherently negative
adverb (e.g. don't hardly) are occasionally used by middle-
class speakers, whereas multiple negatives involving indefinite pronouns (e.g. He didn't do nothing) are categorically absent. In cases where certain subcategories of a
variable reveal the occasional presence of a variant categorically absent in other subcategories, we conclude that a
particular subtype of a variable is somewhat less socially
stigmatized than other subtypes of the variable.

Although middle-class informants are most often characterized by the categorical absence of certain variants of
a grammatical variable, working-class informants do not generally reveal the categorical presence or absence of particular variants. For all the grammatical variables a majority
of working-class informants reveal variation between socially
stigmatized and non-stigmatized variants. As will be seen in
Section 5.5.2, this variation raises certain descriptive
problems concerning the treatment of particular variants in
a grammar of NNE.

The categorical absence of certain variants among middle-
class speakers contrasts with the social differentiation of
phonological variables. For three of the four phonological
variables the differences were quantitative rather than qualitative. If the four phonological and four grammatical variables chosen for this study are indicative of a wider range

of sociolinguistic variables, an important difference in the
social differentiation of phonological and grammatical variables can be suggested, namely, that the social differentiation of phonological variables tends to be quantitative but
the social differentiation of grammatical variables tends to
be qualitative.

A corollary of the above observation is the observation
that grammatical variables more often reveal sharp rather
than gradient stratification (see sec. 4.5.1) between the
different social groups. On the other hand, the phonological
variables more often reveal gradient stratification between
the social groups.

As with the phonological variables, other social factors
regularly intersect with social class to account for observed
differences in speech behavior. In the discussion of the
individual grammatical variables we investigated the factors
of style, sex, age, and racial isolation.

The differences in the frequency with which certain
stigmatized variants occur in the reading and interview style
suggest that there are rather drastic shifts between the two
styles. In part, the relative infrequency of certain stigmatized grammatical variants is attributable to the fact that
there is more conscious awareness of socially diagnostic grammatical variants than there is of phonological variants. For
certain grammatical variants, however, a more important consideration is the fact that certain stigmatized variants could
only occur if the reader substituted an entirely different
word for the form in the text. This means that a sentence in
the reading passage such as I don't think any of my friends ...
would have to be read as I don't think none of my friends ...
to realize a multiple negative in the reading passage. The
substitution of entire words or morphemes is a matter of dialect interference and not stylistic variation. Socially

significant reading interference should not be treated on the same level with stylistic variation.[36] Because the matter of reading interference is involved in several of the grammatical variables, it is difficult to reliably assess the stylistic variation of grammatical variables on the basis of interview and reading style.

The factor of sex intersects in an important way with social class. As with the phonological variables, females generally use socially stigmatized variants less frequently than males. We can thus conclude that for females there are slightly different expectations in speech behavior than there are for males.

Age is an essential factor intersecting with social class to account for speech differences. The adult speech pattern shows considerable difference from both pre-adolescents and teen-agers. This difference is considerably more exaggerated for the grammatical variables than it is for the phonological variables. A slight difference between pre-adolescents and teen-agers is also sometimes observed, but this difference does not nearly approximate the difference between the adults and the two non-adult age grades. In the discussion of age as it correlated with phonological variables, we suggested that for the middle-class pre-adolescents and teen-agers the differences in the frequency with which certain variants occurred was relatively "diverse" when the figures for individual informants were compared. But for the grammatical variables the same observation does not hold true. Middle-class pre-adolescents and teen-agers are more likely to adopt working-class phonological patterns than they are grammatical patterns. For example, several pre-adolescent and teen-age informants reveal scores for the phonological variables which are quite typically working-class, but have no or very infrequent occurrences of multiple negation, invariant be, and

suffixal -Z absence. For whatever reason the middle-class
pre-adolescent or teen-ager adopts working-class phonological
features (e.g. peer identity, reaction to adult norms, etc.),
this type of selectivity coincides with the observation that
grammatical variables are generally more social diagnostic
than phonological variables.

A final factor investigated was racial isolation. Although racial isolation helps to explain certain individual
cases in which socially stigmatized variants occur among
middle-class pre-adolescent and teen-age informants, it does
not have as great an effect as it does for the phonological
variables. The fact that a UMN pre-adolescent or teen-ager
may have predominantly Negro contacts does not give assurance
that one can necessarily expect socially stigmatized grammatical variants.

5.5.2 The Linguistic Function of the Grammatical Variable

In addition to our examination of the social function of the
grammatical variables the linguistic function of the variants
has been described in terms of a NNE grammatical construct.
Several general conclusions can be suggested on this basis.

In the first place, several of the variables revealed
the intersection of a grammatical and phonological pattern.
In invariant be, for example, two of the three underlying
sources realize be because of a phonological rather than a
grammatical pattern. Similarly, there is important phonological patterning which must be appealed to in order to
account for the operation of copula zero realization. Labov,
in fact, has suggested that copula zero realization should
be treated entirely as a phonological rather than a grammatical pattern. Even if one does not go as far as Labov it
is difficult to deny the important intersection of a phonological with a grammatical pattern for copula zero realization.

Another matter which has constantly faced us is the
question of whether certain grammatical variants can be considered an integral part of the NNE grammatical system. If
we were dealing with variants which were categorically absent
in the majority of our working-class informants, the answer
would be simple. But, in most cases, the working-class
speakers fluctuate between variants. Although it is tempt-
ing to treat any form which occurs in an informant's speech
as an integral part of his system, certain forms in working-
class speech are considered importations from a socially
superordinate and prestigious SE dialect. On the one hand,
the relative infrequency of certain variants suggests that
these are not actually a part of the basic NNE system. Certainly the position of NNE as a dialect socially subordinate
to SE is the type of situation in which one can expect considerable dialect importation from SE. Especially in any
semi-formal situation such as the interview, a certain amount
of dialect borrowing from superimposed SE norm will occur.
On the other hand, structural clues of unfamiliarity with
certain variants also suggest that a form is being borrowed
from a SE dialect. Certain types of hypercorrection are the
most revealing evidence of structural unfamiliarity with the
rules governing the realization patterns of particular forms.
The most outstanding example of this type of hypercorrection
is found in the use of third person singular -Z (see sec. 5.1).

For most of the variables the question is whether or not
an SE form can be considered a part of the NNE grammatical
system. But for invariant be the trend is reversed. That is,
a particular variant which is found in NNE, namely 'distributive be', is a marked grammatical category which does not
correspond to any known grammatical category in SE.

We have already observed that extra-linguistic factors
have important constraints on the variability of grammatical

forms. But as with the phonological variables, it is necessary to isolate independent linguistic variables which affect
the variability of grammatical items. Certain syntactical
environments such as the preceding and following phrase favor
the realization of particular grammatical forms more than
others. It is essential to observe the uniform and regular
effect of particular independent linguistic factors as well
as extra-linguistic facts in order to take into account the
fully systematic nature of variability for grammatical items.

NOTES

1. -Z also functions as an adverbial marker in items such
   as sometimes, nowadays, etc. Adverbial -Z is also absent
   in the speech of some Negroes, but this will not be considered in the present analysis.

2. Dillard (1968: 2) maintains that the absence of -Z in a
   form such as he do "is NOT simply a grammatical equivalent of he does, differing only in a 'dropped' inflec-
   tional ending." In this formal linguistic analysis no
   motivation is found for his position.

3. In narrative discourse, -Z also occurs on non-third person singular forms for white nonstandard speakers in
   Detroit. This usage is different from its occurrence
   among Negro speakers in two important ways. First, there
   is no absence of third person singular forms for the
   whites. Second, -Z on non-third person singular forms
   is limited to narrative style among whites whereas it
   is not stylistically restricted for the Negroes.

4. The "degree of deviation" is formally defined as the
   number of structural features (e.g. construction type,
   person, number, etc.) not shared by the correct and the
   hypercorrect construction.

5. Ralph W. Fasold (personal conversation) reports a number
   of instances of this type of hypercorrection on the
   basis of a test designed specifically to elicit possessives. Fasold also reports that -Z possessive sometimes
   occurs on both proper nouns, so that one occasionally
   finds constructions such as Alvin's Jackson's car.

In this corpus there are very few constructions of this type, so that no actual instances of this hypercorrection are found.

6. The symbol ⇔ is used to refer to what Gleason (1965: 199) calls a relationship of agnation. This relationship takes place when two or more sentences structurally different are realizations of the same underlying source.

7. There are several types of constructions in which multiple negation is quite permissible in SE. For example, there is only one underlying negative in the SE sentence He didn't go to the store, I don't think, yet the negative is realized in both clauses. This type of multiple negation (which only occurs with a small set of verbs including believe, think, imagine, suspect, etc.) is related to linear order of the base and embedded clause. (Note that the negative is only realized once in I don't think he went to the store.) Multiple negation of this type was not considered with other types of multiple negation in this analysis. For a discussion of negation in SE, see Klima (1964).

8. Since it is also possible to place emphatic stress on nothing when multiple negation occurs, the surface contrast can be neutralized, in which case ambiguity arises.

9. Some of these types of multiple negation do occur among white Southern nonstandard speakers.

10. Labov, et al. (1968: 272) suggest that there are two dialects of white nonstandard English, one in which this type of construction is unacceptable and the other in which it is acceptable.

11. It is possible, particularly when ain't is the auxiliary, to suggest that there are two underlying clauses which are the source of this construction. Thus, the sentence Ain't none of us hard-headed may be realized from the same underlying source as It ain't none of us tha's hard-headed (for a discussion of this, see Labov, et al. (1968: 284-286)).

12. The distinction between specific and generic determiners cuts across the traditional distinction between "definite" and "indefinite".

13. The implication of this statement for a grammatical construct of NNE is that a in a negative sentence differs

qualitatively from <u>no</u> (<u>He ain't hit a policeman</u> ≠ <u>He ain't hit no policeman</u>).

14. For a discussion of why some forms tend to be retained in the form they appear in the reading while others are affected by "dialect interference", see Shuy, "A Linguistic Background for Developing Beginning Reading Materials for Black Children" (1969).

15. The absence of copula and auxiliary <u>be</u> will be treated together, since the same pattern is operating for both. Most descriptions of English syntax separate the two grammatical functions of <u>be</u>. (For a treatment of the two functions in terms of one grammatical pattern, see Bach 1967). In the remainder of this section the term copula absence is used to refer to both copula and auxiliary absence.

16. The use of the word "regularly" does not mean that the copula always occurs in some of these environments. For example, isolated examples of copula absence in a past tense context can be found; similarly, there are instances of copula absence with first person singular forms. For other environments, however, such as non-finite copula and tag questions, no examples of absence are ever found. There are two levels of ungrammaticality found in the above list -- one in which copula/ auxiliary absence is never found (Numbers 3, 4, 5, 6) and one in which infrequent occurrences of copula absence are found (Numbers 1, 2, 7). The first type of ungrammaticality involves grammatical constraints and the second type phonological constraints (see Labov 1968: 9).

17. From Labov's theoretical viewpoint, that of transformational-generative grammar, copula absence is viewed as "deletion" operating on a contracted form (i.e. in the ordered sequence of rules contraction necessarily precedes deletion). From the viewpoint underlying the present analysis, copula absence is considered a matter of "zero realization".

18. Actually, there are several exceptions to this correspondence involving the lexical items <u>what's</u>, <u>that's</u>, <u>it's</u>, and lexical items ending in a sibilant (e.g. <u>fish</u>, <u>rose</u>). In the former case, NNE does not regularly have zero realization, but SE contracts; in the latter case, NNE has zero realization, but SE does not contract when <u>is</u> follows. For an explanation of these exceptions in

terms of phonological environment, see Labov (1968: 37-41). These apparent exceptions to the NNE correspondence of zero realization for SE contraction do not detract from the overwhelming regularity with which this correspondence occurs.

19. The percentage of full forms, although not explicitly given, is easily derived by subtracting the total of contraction plus zero realization from 100 per cent.

20. Although is occasionally occurs with non-third person singular forms, the converse, are occurring with third person singular forms (e.g. *He are good), is not found.

21. Labov (1968: 5) correctly points out that the question of an underlying copula in NNE should not be confused with the question of the level on which the copula should be introduced in SE or NNE. For example, from a transformational-generative viewpoint, one may introduce the copula by a phrase structure rule (see Chomsky 1965: 107) or by a transformational rule (see Bach 1967: 468).

22. The phonemes /s/ and /z/, of course, are simply morphophonemic alternants, /z/ occurring following voiced segments (e.g. /hiyz biziy/ 'he's busy'), and /s/ following voiceless segments (e.g. /jæks biziy/ 'Jack's busy').

23. Although /r/ is generally reduced to /ə/, a rule which results in the zero realization of /ə/ removes any "phonological vestige" of /r/, according to Labov's interpretation.

24. An underlying word boundary refers to a grammatical word as opposed to a phonological word.

25. The term "invariant be" suggested by Labov, et al. (1968: 228) seems to be the most acceptable term for referring to all occurrences of the form be where one might expect am, are, or is in SE.

26. In the total count both conjugated forms of the copula be (sometimes he's busy) and present tense forms of noncopula verbs (e.g. sometimes, he goes to the movies) are included. Of all the adverbs which do not co-occur with invariant be, only 12 of the 321 co-occur with the conjugated form of the copula.

27. The category "usual occurrence" combines Crystal's cate-
    gories "usual" and "regular" occurrence since no formal
    motivation for distinguishing these types has been found.

28. The observation that be in a future context may be the
    realization of underlying will be is not to say that
    will functions strictly as a marker of futurity. Joos
    (1964: 156) suggests that will means that there is
    "adequate assurance of eventual occurrence."

29. Fasold's test, not reported in his present study "Tense
    and the form 'be' in Black English" (forthcoming), will
    be described as part of a final report of the Washington
    Dialect Study.

30. Joos (1964: 173) suggests that would means "remote
    assurance of eventual occurrence."

31. Feigenbaum (forthcoming) suggests that a sentence such
    as He be my brother should not be considered ungram-
    matical because it would be acceptable "if the speaker,
    from time to time, proclaimed his brotherhood, but at
    other times, was not sure of his loyalty." In a spe-
    cialized context such as Feigenbaum suggests, the sen-
    tence may be acceptable; however, the claim that be
    cannot be used in reference to a permanent relationship
    is unaffected by Feigenbaum's observation.

32. These analyses of be are all taken from pre-publication
    manuscripts to be included in Current Viewpoints Toward
    Non-Standard 'Be' (Shuy and Fasold, eds.).

33. Although it can be inferred that this construction is
    ungrammatical NNE on the basis of this study, William A.
    Stewart reports (personal conversation) that a number of
    his Negro informants in Washington, D.C. have accepted
    this as a grammatical NNE sentence.

34. This type of count assumes that approximately the same
    types of narrative and same amount of discourse are
    elicited from each informant to insure comparability.
    Although there is considerable variation in what each
    informant talks about, the interviews, for the most
    part, are sufficiently similar to reveal the social dis-
    tribution of the informants on the basis of this vari-
    able.

35. The important observation concerning will be is that it
    is "unmarked" with reference to the frequency with which

an activity occurs. That is, it may be used with reference to a single occurrence (e.g. He'll be here just once)
or repeated occurrence of an activity (e.g. He'll usually
be here in the afternoon).

36. One effort to view some of the matters of reading inter-
     ference for NNE speakers is found in Teaching Black
     Children To Read (Baratz and Shuy, eds. 1969).

6 CONCLUSION

6.1 Summary of Principal Conclusions

The primary goal of this study was to describe the correlation of linguistic variables with the social variables of
status, sex, age, racial isolation, and style in the speech
of Detroit Negroes. Each of these social variables correlates
with linguistic variation.

Social Status: Social status is the single most important variable correlating with linguistic differences. Of the four
social classes which have been delimited in this study, the
most clear-cut linguistic boundary is found between the lower-
middle and upper-working social classes and the least clear-
cut difference between upper-working and lower-working classes.
According to Landecker (1960: 874), it is most difficult to
determine sharp social boundaries at the lower end of the
social scale. We thus observe that the least clear-cut linguistic boundary parallels the least clear-cut social boundary.
    Of the three individual scales which comprise the overall
social status scale, the linguistic differentiation correlates
more consistently with differences on the education and occupation scales than with the residency scale. On the education
and occupation scales, the upper-middle, lower-middle, and
upper-working classes are clearly differentiated from each
other, but there is minimal difference between the upper-
working and lower-working classes. The residency scale, on

214

the other hand, reveals slight differentiation between the
first three social classes (i.e. upper-middle, lower-middle,
and upper-working), but considerable difference between the
upper-working and lower-working classes. Thus, the social
differentiation of linguistic variables coincides with differences on the education and occupation scales, but not on
the residency scales. One can conclude that residency differences of Detroit Negroes are less reliable in estimating
linguistic differences than occupation and education differences.

Sex: Within each social class it is observed that females
generally approximate the standard English norm more than
males do. Hannerz (1967: 2) has observed that the Negro
male departs more from the mainstream norm of middle-class
behavior than the female. The sex differentiation of speech
behavior in this study parallels Hannerz' general observation.

Age: Age also correlates with differences in speech behavior.
Adults generally use socially stigmatized variants less than
teen-agers and pre-adolescents. Although it was hypothesized
at the outset of this study that teen-agers might reveal less
frequent usage of stigmatized forms than pre-adolescents,
this is not regularly observed. The most obvious reason for
this is the explicit rejection of adult norms by teen-agers.

A comparison of the individual informants with each other
indicates that there is more individual variation among middle-
class pre-adolescents and teen-agers than among middle-class
adults. Middle-class adults are relatively consistent in their
use of standard English, whereas some pre-adolescents and
teen-agers show considerable divergence from the standard
English norm. On the other hand, there is more individual
variation among working-class adults than pre-adolescents and

teen-agers. Some of these adults approximate the standard
English norm more than others, whereas the working-class
pre-adolescents and teen-agers are relatively consistent in
their use of Nonstandard Negro English.

Style: There is considerable variation based on the differentiation of interview and reading style, the latter style
consistently showing a closer approximation to the standard
English norm. This stylistic variation indicates that the
informants recognize (whether consciously or unconsciously)
that particular variables are markers of social status. The
more stylistic variation there is, the more socially "marked"
the linguistic variable. Both working-class and lower-middle
class informants have more stylistic variation than the upper-
middle class informants.

Racial Isolation: The factor of racial isolation is useful
only in comparing the speech of a number of upper-middle class
informants who have integrated or predominantly white contacts
with the speech of upper-middle class informants having predominantly Negro contacts. Racial isolation has some effect
on the speech of pre-adolescents and teen-agers, but there is
very little effect on adults.

In addition to the correlation of linguistic with social variables, several aspects of the nature of the linguistic variables have been considered, including: (1) the extent to which
the social differentiation of linguistic variables is quantitative or qualitative; (2) the relation between socially diagnostic phonological and grammatical variables; and (3) the
effect of independent linguistic constraints on variability.

The investigation of phonological and grammatical variables reveals that the phonological differences between social groups tend to be quantitative whereas the grammatical differences are often qualitative. Three of the four phonological variables (word-final consonant clusters, syllable-final d, and postvocalic r) indicate that the social groups are differentiated primarily on the basis of the relative frequency of variants. Only the θ variable, which shows the categorical absence of the f variant in middle-class speech, indicates a qualitative difference between social groups. On the other hand, all four grammatical variables (multiple negation, suffixal -Z, copula absence, and invariant be) reveal the categorical absence of certain variants among middle-class informants.

By introducing the concepts of "sharp" (i.e. a significant difference in the frequency of particular variants between contiguous social groups) and "gradient" (i.e. a progressive difference in the frequency of particular variants between social groups) we have suggested an important difference in the way phonological and grammatical variables stratify the population. Grammatical variables usually show sharp stratification, whereas phonological variables show gradient stratification. All the grammatical variables investigated in this study reveal sharp stratification, whereas three of the four phonological variables indicate gradient stratification.

Finally, this research has demonstrated that it is impossible to arrive at an adequate understanding of the nature of sociolinguistic variation without considering the effects of independent linguistic constraints. In accounting for frequency differences among variants it is essential to consider the effect of linguistic environment. For example, whether the following environment is consonantal or non-consonantal has a significant effect on the relative frequency with which the final member of a word-final consonant cluster is absent.

The effect of a non-consonantal environment in reducing the
frequency of absence is uniform for all informants regardless of status, age, sex, style, and racial isolation. The
linguistic constraints on variability can be viewed in terms
of an hierarchy -- each constraint in the hierarchy outranks
the effects of all constraints below it in the hierarchy.
For example, in the consideration of the postvocalic r variable, it is evident that the distinction between a preceding
central versus a non-central vowel in a stressed syllable has
a greater effect on r absence than the distinction between a
following vocalic or non-vocalic environment. It is the
intersection of independent linguistic with social factors
that accounts for speech variation in a systematic and regular way.

6.2   Implications for Further Research

The sociolinguistic description of the speech of Detroit
Negroes raises a number of issues which need further investigation. Both from the point of view of Detroit Negro speech
and the sociolinguistic model used in this study, there are
unanswered questions and unexplored areas.

There is a need to expand the sample and check the find-
ings of this study with a wider representation of the population, particularly with reference to age, sex, and racial
isolation. Furthermore, the functional reasons for sex and
age differences must be considered. Is the pattern of sex
differentiation due to different types of contact situations
that males and females have with the socially superordinate
white community (e.g. female domestics working in close contact with middle-class white females) or is this an indigenous
behavioral characteristic of the Negro community (e.g. the
use of socially stigmatized forms is a symbol of masculinity)?
Only an analysis of the types of social contact Negroes have

with the middle-class white community and a thorough ethno-
graphic description of sex roles in the Negro community can
determine the source of this sex differentiation. Likewise,
it is necessary to study age-grading in the Negro community
to determine why the speech behavior of pre-adolescents and
teen-agers is distinct from the adults. Although it has been
suggested that teen-agers may speak differently from adults
because of their explicit rejection of adult norms, this can
be verified or repudiated only on the basis of extensive
description of the functional role of speech in peer group
identity among Negroes. Such studies must include the value
systems of homogeneous peer groups.

An increasingly important area for future sociolinguistic
research is the role of Nonstandard Negro English in relation
to the present mood of "black consciousness" in the Negro
community. At present, the emphasis on the Afro-American
heritage of Negroes has not recognized the distinct history
of American Negro speech. At this point, the research of
Shuy, Baratz and Wolfram (1969) indicates that working-class
Negroes who use socially stigmatized speech forms often have
the same low opinion of such forms as middle-class speakers
who do not use them. If dialectal pride in Nonstandard Negro
English results from the current emphasis on black identity,
the functional role of Nonstandard Negro English will be
drastically restructured.

The relation of Nonstandard Negro English to standard
English as it compares with other language contact situations
still has not been investigated. For example, is the relation
of these two language varieties a "diglossic" situation as
Ferguson (1959) has elaborated the concept, or is it simply a
nonstandard-standard relation? Further studies must consider
the functional relation of standard English and Nonstandard
Negro English in terms of the entire spectrum of American
social and racial relations.

The results of this study should be compared with those from other large urban areas. Although exploratory comparisons with the structure of the speech by Negroes in Washington, D.C. and New York City suggest that there are many similarities in Negro speech in these cities, objective evidence is still needed to conclude that the speech situation in Detroit is typical of most Northern cities. The speech patterns of Southern Negroes must also be compared with those in the North to determine the extent to which these two varieties actually are similar and different. In the South, the speech of Negroes must be compared to that of whites of a comparable socioeconomic class. Until such research is carried out, the current controversy concerning the relationship of white Southern and Negro speech cannot be resolved. A comparison of Negro and Southern white speech may also shed considerable light on the historical origin of Nonstandard Negro English.

Another area for investigation is the relation of phonological and grammatical variables in social differentiation. In this study it was noted that phonological variables tended to reveal quantitative differences and grammatical variables qualitative differences. The generalizability of this observation can be validated or repudiated only as more variables are examined. Furthermore, results based on quantitative measurement should be subjected to the calculation of statistical significance if the results are to be considered more than suggestive.

A final area for investigation is Labov's concept of the variable rule. Although the actual formulation of variable rules was outside the scope of this study, this is one of the most fertile areas for further sociolinguistic research. The suggestion that variable rules may be incorporated into a formal language description has important implications for theoretical linguistics and is an issue on which the insights of sociolinguistics and theoretical linguistics can merge.

APPENDIX A : List of Informants

Upper-Middle Class White Informants

Tape No.	Age	Sex
19	11	M
29	14	F
43	41	F
88	41	F
122	15	F
123	11	F
160	12	M
161	48	M
171	10	F
236	42	M
528	15	M
650	17	M

Upper-Middle Class Negro Informants

Tape No.	Age	Sex
72	41	M
328	17	M
358	48	M
690	38	F
705	47	F
707	11	M
709	14	F
710	17	F
711	10	F
712	10	F
718	14	M
726	11	M

Lower-Middle Class Negro Informants

Tape No.	Age	Sex
55	52	F
134	46	M
141	16	F

221

228	11	F
293	37	M
651	42	F
714	16	M
720	17	M
723	17	F
724	11	M
725	10	M

Upper-Working Class Negro Informants

Tape No.	Age	Sex
193	12	F
208	31	F
305	35	M
318	15	F
330	49	M
461	11	M
478	15	F
487	12	F
521	10	M
526	16	M
569	30	F
586	17	M

Lower-Working Class Negro Informants

Tape No.	Age	Sex
214	32	F
278	16	F
304	17	M
369	12	M
370	10	F
444	12	F
447	53	M
481	37	F
489	11	M
506	48	M
565	14	F
583	17	M

APPENDIX B : Detroit Dialect Study Questionnaire

I. GAMES AND LEISURE (10 minutes)

    A. What kinds of games do you play around here? (perhaps marbles, Red Rover, Kick-the-Can, May-I, Capture the Flag, Hide and Seek, game with bottle caps)

        1. Note each game and ask about how each is played, number of players, etc.

        2. Get terms for "goal," "home," "when a new person comes," "getting in free," how you decide who is IT, use of rhymes. (also get marbles, jacks, hop-scotch, jump rope, tackle-tackle, pom pom, roof tag)

    B. What are your favorite TV programs? (theaters, movies) (elicit recent episode on Batman, UNCLE, etc.)

    C. Do you have a pet? Tell me about it.

    D. Is there any way you can get a wish? (elicit eye lashes, chicken bone, or tooth comes out)

II. SCHOOL (10 minutes)

    A. Tell me about your school? What do you study? (get geography, history, arithmetic, etc.)

        1. From your seat in class, tell me what you can see. (get blackboard, desk, chair)

        2. If you walk outside the classroom, where are you? (hall) What's in it? (fountain, lockers, stairs)

        3. What's outside the school? (playground, horse, swings, teeter totter, monkey bars [define])

        4. What do kids do after school is out? (from Negroes, get rippin' and runnin')

    B. Did you ever have a teacher who hollered a lot? What about? Did you ever get yelled at? Was it your fault?

    C. Can you tell me about the best teacher you ever had? Who was she? Why did you like her?

    D. Did you ever have a teacher you just couldn't stand? What

was there about her that you didn't like? Did the kids in
your class really "trick" your teacher last year?

E. Who was the smartest kid in your class? What did he do that
was so good? What favors or rewards does the smart kid get?

F. Who was the dumbest kid? What did he do that was dumb? What
does the teacher do to dumb kids?

G. What time do you get out of school? (or, What time does it
start?) (get quarter till, of, to _____)

III. GROUP STRUCTURE (10 minutes)

A. For child: Is there a bunch of guys you always hang around
               with and do stuff with?

    For adult: Is there a group of people you used to (asso-
               ciate) with?

    1. About how old are they? (Were/are they about the same
        age?)

    2. Child: And you're _____ (how old)?
        Adult: Are they still the same ones? Do you still see
                them a lot? If not, who?

    3. Do· any of the guys (people) speak Polish? Spanish?
        Hungarian, etc.?

    4. Are there any Negro (white, Jewish) kids (people) in
        your bunch (group)?

B. In your bunch (group), is there one guy (person) that
    everybody listens to (regards as leader)?

    1. Why? (smartest, biggest, etc.)

    2. Can new kids get into your bunch? How?

C. What do you want to be when you finish school? (What did
    you hope to be when you were younger?) How long does it
    take to become a _____? What does a _____ do?
    If you could do it all over again, what would you want to be?
    If you had all the money you could ever want, all the money
    in the world, what would you do with it?

D. Your job (for men or working women). Describe what you do
    in a day's work. (try to get specialized vocabulary of the
    occupation) Where do you work? _____

E. Neighborhood

    1. What do they call this part of town?

    2. What are the boundaries? _____

    3. What is this city called? _____ (if
        necessary by now)

    4. What are some streets in Detroit? What about the <u>big</u>
        ones?

        a. The one that goes to East Detroit? (Gratiot)
        b. The one that goes by the University of Detroit?
            (Livernois)
        c. Down by Cobo Hall is _____? (Fort Street)
        d. The one that Hudson's is on? (Woodward) (get
            others, too) Get expressways or freeways, too
            (Ford, Lodge, Chrysler)

    5. Where were you born? _____

    6. Where else have you lived in Detroit?

    7. Where else have you lived outside of Detroit?

    8. Where have you gone on trips?

F. Special Occasions

    1. How does your family celebrate the holidays? (for Jewish
        kids -- Bar Mitzvah; for Jewish girls -- Baz Mitzvah)
        (Catholics -- first communion) (elicit family or group
        customs and terms, especially religious elements, special
        cooking, gifts, etc.)

    2. What would you like for Christmas this year? (if a bike,
        etc., describe it) What was the best Christmas you ever
        got? (Jewish holiday -- Hanukkah)

    3. What do you do on October 31? (elicit pumpkins, Hallo-
        ween, witch)

        a. When you ring the doorbell, what do you say?
        b. Tell me about your costume last year. If you had
            your choice, what would you choose this year?

IV. FIGHTING, ACCIDENTS AND ILLNESS (10 minutes)

    A. What kinds of things do fights usually start about around
        here?

1. Are there rules for a fair fight? (When is it over?
    Does the loser say "uncle", "I give"?)
    (IF you get nothing above)
    If you saw someone kicking someone else on the ground
    (or using a stick, or a chain, or a lead pipe, etc.)
    and it was supposed to be a fair fight, what would you
    do?

2. Did you ever see anyone get beat up real bad? What
    happened to him?

3. Did you ever get into a fight with a guy bigger than
    you? What happened?

4. Do the guys usually fight one-against-one or in gangs?
    What are the rules for gang fights?

B. Have you ever been in the hospital?

    1. What is the worst illness you have ever had? Describe
        it (and others).

    2. When a person starts to sneeze or cough, you might say
        he is _____ (catching, taking) a cold.

C. Have you ever been in an automobile accident? (or, Tell
    me the worst one you ever saw -- draw out details).

D. Were you ever in a situation where you thought you might be
    killed or die?
    After response, ask: Sometimes people say whatever is going
    to happen is going to happen. How do you feel about that?

READING PASSAGE*

NOBODY KNOWS YOUR NAME

Last year I went out for the basketball team, and I made out
better than I expected. I wasn't too big, but I was quick on my
feet, and my jump shot used to drop in when it counted. The coach
told me himself I was a real help to the school.

---

*The following reading passage was originally constructed by William
Labov in such a way as to incorporate a number of phonological variables. Although the passage reads as a coherent narrative, items
were specifically included to elicit reading style pronunciation of
particular features.

But you couldn't tell that to Eleanor. No matter if I did good or bad, she'd ask me after every game: "Why can't _you_ be the man to put it in the basket?" I'd tell her, "Look, Eleanor, everybody can't be a star. I'm not a forward; I'm not a center; I'm a guard. I play the back court."

"But you passed it to Lester again," she used to say, "you must have passed it to Lester sixty times, and he missed it most of the time. Why don't _you_ make the shots?" "It's easy enough to explain," I told her, "if you only know what's what. Lester is seven-foot-two; I'm five-foot-ten. He just twists his wrist and puts it in."

She wouldn't see it, and I couldn't make her see it. I'd talk till I was out of breath, but I might as well have kept my mouth shut. It was always something: if it wasn't this thing, it was that thing, or the other thing. I'd tell her again, "Look Eleanor, I'm a guard. I play the back court."

Then she tried a new line. "I know you're right," she said. "But what about my pride? I don't think any of my friends remember if you're a center or an end or a tackle. Nobody knows your name!"

She made my blood boil. I said I wasn't going to hog the ball to please her. I was ready for murder or worse. And she said she wouldn't go out with me any more if I didn't score a lot of points. So I told the coach about it. He said, "Artie, everybody can't be a star. You're a good team man. It should be an easy game tomorrow night, so we'll keep setting you up."

They fixed me up to look good all right. I just hung under the basket, and everybody passed me the ball. I pushed the easy ones in, and nobody noticed when I missed. By the end of the game, I had thrown in thirty-three points. The whole school was cheering for me: Everybody was shouting my name.

Everybody that is, but Eleanor. I looked for her here, there, everywhere -- but there wasn't hide nor hair of her. Finally I called her father on the phone. "I just made thirty-three points, Mr. Jones -- but I can't find Eleanor. Do you know where she is?"

Her father said, "Just a minute." Then he said, "She says she can't come to the phone right now, son. She's watching the Dave Clark Five on Channel 2. But she says, will you please do it for her again next week -- she can watch you then."

Next year I'm going out for the swimming team -- under water. Down there, nobody -- but nobody -- is going to know my name.

BIBLIOGRAPHY

Bach, Emmon
1967   "Have and be in English Syntax", Language 43:462-485.

Bailey, Beryl Loftman
1964   "A Proposal for the Study of the Grammar of Negro English
        in New York City", Project Literacy Reports No. 2.   Ithaca,
        Cornell University.

1965a   "Toward a New Perspective in Negro English Dialectology",
        American Speech 40:171-177.

1965b   Jamaican Creole Syntax.   London, Cambridge University Press.

1968   "Some Aspects of the Impact of Linguistics on Language
        Teaching in Disadvantaged Communities", Elementary English
        45:570-577.

Baratz, Joan C. and Roger W. Shuy, eds.
1969   Teaching Black Children to Read, Washington, D.C., Center
        for Applied Linguistics.

Bernstein, Basil B.
1960   "Language and Social Class", British Journal of Sociology
        11:271-276.

1962   "Social Class, Linguistic Codes and Grammatical Elements",
        Language and Speech 5:221-240.

1964   "Elaborated and Restricted Codes: Their Social Origins and
        Some Consequences", in The Ethnography of Communication,
        American Anthropologist 66, No. 6, Part 2:55-69.

1966   "Elaborated and Restricted Codes: An Outline", Socio-
        logical Inquiry 36:254-259.

Bloch, Bernard
1941   "Phonemic Overlapping", American Speech 16:278-284.

Board of Education, Detroit, Michigan
1965   "Racial Isolation of Students and Contract Personnel in
        the Detroit Public Schools".   Detroit, Mimeographed.

Bright, William
1960   "Linguistic Change in Some Indian Caste Dialects", in
        Linguistic Diversity in South Asia, ed. by Charles A.
        Ferguson and John J. Gumperz.   Bloomington, Indiana University.

1966   "Introduction: The Dimensions of Sociolinguistics", in
         Sociolinguistics, ed. by William Bright. The Hague,
         Mouton & Co.

Bright, William and A.K. Ramanujan
   1964   "Sociolinguistic Variation and Language Change", in Proceed-
         ings of the 9th International Congress of Linguists. The
         Hague, Mouton & Co.

Chomsky, Noam
   1962   "Current Issues in Linguistic Theory", in The Structure of
         Language: Readings in the Philosophy of Language, ed. by
         Jerry A. Fodor and Jerrold J. Katz. Englewood Cliffs, N.J.,
         Prentice-Hall.

   1965   Aspects of the Theory of Syntax. Cambridge, Mass., M.I.T.
         Press.

Crystal, David
   1966   "Specification and English Tenses", Journal of Linguistics
         2:1-34.

The Detroit Area Study
   1956   A Social Profile of Detroit. Ann Arbor, University of
         Michigan.

   1960   The Detroit Area Study: A Bibliography Based on Detroit
         Area Study Research. Ann Arbor, University of Michigan.

Dillard, J.L.
   1967   "Negro Children's Dialect in the Inner City", The Florida
         FL Reporter 5, No. 3:7-10.

   1968   "Non-Standard Negro Dialects -- Convergence or Divergence".
         Jamaica, Unpublished paper given at the Conference on
         Pidginization and Creolization of Languages.

Ellis, Robert A.
   1957   "Social Stratification and Social Relations: An Empirical
         Test of the Disjunctiveness of Social Classes", American
         Sociological Review 22:570-578.

Ervin-Tripp, Susan M.
   1964   "An Analysis of the Interaction of Language, and Listener",
         in The Ethnography of Communication, American Anthropologist
         66, No. 6, Part 2:86-102.

Fasold, Ralph W.
   1967   "Two Fricatives in Black English: A Generative Phonology
         Approach", Washington, D.C., Center for Applied Linguistics,
         Mimeographed.

forthcoming   "Tense and the Form 'be' in Black English", in
        Current Viewpoints on Nonstandard 'Be', ed. by Roger W.
        Shuy and Ralph W. Fasold. Washington, D.C., Center for
        Applied Linguistics.

Feigenbaum, Irwin W.
   forthcoming   "Two Oppositions in the Verb System of Negro Non-
        standard English", in Current Viewpoints on Nonstandard 'Be',
        ed. by Roger W. Shuy and Ralph W. Fasold. Washington, D.C.,
        Center for Applied Linguistics.

Ferguson, Charles A.
   1959   "Diglossia", Word 15:325-340.

   1968   "Absence of Copula in Normal Speech, Baby Talk, and Pidgins".
        Jamaica, Unpublished paper given at the Conference on
        Pidginization and Creolization of Languages.

Ferguson, Charles A. and John J. Gumperz, eds.
   1960   Linguistic Diversity in South Asia: Studies in Regional,
        Social and Functional Variation. Bloomington, Indiana
        University.

Fisher, John L.
   1958   "Social Influences on the Choice of a Linguistic Variant",
        Word 14:47-56.

Francis, W. Nelson
   1958   The Structure of American English. New York, The Ronald
        Press.

Gleason, H.A., Jr.
   1961   An Introduction to Descriptive Linguistics, Rev. ed.
        New York, Holt, Rinehart & Winston.

   1964   "The Organization of Language: A Stratificational View", in
        Monograph Series on Languages and Linguistics, Vol. 17,
        ed. by C.I.J.M. Stuart. Washington, D.C., Georgetown
        University Press.

   1965   Linguistics and English Grammar. New York, Holt, Rinehart
        & Winston.

Gumperz, John J.
   1958a   "Dialect Differences and Social Stratification in a North
        Indian Village", American Anthropologist 60:668-681.

   1958b   "Phonological Differences in Three Hindi Village Dialects",
        Language 34:212-224.

   1961   "Speech Variation and the Study of Indian Civilization",
        American Anthropologist 63:976-988.

1964   "Linguistic and Social Interaction in Two Communities", in
        The Ethnography of Communication, American Anthropologist
        66, No. 6, Part 2:137-153.

Gumperz, John J. and C.A. Naim
1960   "Formal and Informal Standards in the Hindi Regional Lan-
        guage Area", Linguistic Diversity in South Asia, ed. by
        Charles A. Ferguson and John J. Gumperz. Bloomington,
        Indiana University.

Hale, Austin
1964   "Disambiguation of the English Article". Grand Forks,
        Unpublished paper delivered at the Summer Institute of
        Linguistics.

Hannerz, Ulf
1967   "Another Look at Lower-Class Negro Sex Roles". Washington,
        D.C., Unpublished paper delivered at the 66th Annual Meet-
        ing of the American Anthropological Association.

Herskovits, Melvil
1941   The Myth of the Negro Past. New York, Harper & Brothers.

Hockett, Charles F.
1950   "Age-Grading and Linguistic Continuity", Language 27:449-557.

Hodges, Luther H. and William L. Batt, Jr.
1964   Negro-White Differences in Geographic Mobility. Washington,
        D.C., U.S. Government Printing Office.

Hollingshead, August B. and F.C. Redlich
1958   Social Class and Mental Illness: A Community Study. New
        York, John Wiley.

Hymes, Dell H.
1962   "The Ethnography of Speaking", in Anthropology and Human
        Behavior, ed. by Thomas Gladwin and William C. Sturtevant.
        Washington, D.C., Anthropological Society of Washington.

1964   "Introduction: Toward Ethnographies of Communication", in
        The Ethnography of Communication, American Anthropologist 66,
        No. 6, Part 2:1-34.

Joos, Martin
1962   The Five Clocks. IJAL Memoir 22. Bloomington, Indiana
        University.

1964   The English Verb. Madison, University of Wisconsin Press.

Klima, Edward S.
1964   "Negation in English", in The Structure of Language: Read-
        ings in the Philosophy of Language, ed. by Jerry A. Fodor
        and Jerrold J. Katz. Englewood Cliffs, Prentice-Hall.

Kurath, Hans
1939   Handbook of the Linguistic Geography of New England. Pro-
        vidence, American Council of Learned Societies.

1949   A Word Geography of the Eastern United States. Ann Arbor,
        University of Michigan Press.

Kurath, Hans, ed.
1941   Linguistic Atlas of New England. Providence, American
        Council of Learned Societies.

Labov, William
1964a   "Phonological Correlates of Social Strattification", in
        The Ethnography of Communication, American Anthropologist 66,
        No. 6, Part 2:164-176.

1964b   "Stages in the Acquisition of Standard English", in Social
        Dialects and Language Learning, ed. by Roger W. Shuy.
        Champaign, National Council of Teachers of English.

1965   "On the Mechanism of Linguistic Change", Monograph Series
        on Languages and Linguistics, Vol. 18, ed. by Charles W.
        Kreidler. Washington, D.C., Georgetown University Press.

1966a   The Social Stratification of English in New York City.
        Washington, D.C., Center for Applied Linguistics.

1966b   "The Linguistic Variable as a Structural Unit", Washington
        Linguistics Review 3:4-22.

1966c   "The Effect of Social Mobility on Linguistic Behavior",
        Sociological Inquiry 36:186-203.

1967   "Some Sources of Reading Problems for Negro Speakers of
        Nonstandard English", in New Directions in Elementary English,
        ed. by Alexander Frazier. Champaign, National Council of
        Teachers of English. [Reprinted with additions and correc-
        tions in Baratz and Shuy 1969.]

1968   "Contraction, Deletion, and Inherent Variation of the
        English Copula". Jamaica, Unpublished paper given at the
        Conference on Pidginization and Creolization of Languages.

Labov, William and Paul Cohen
1967   "Systematic Relations of Standard and Non-Standard Rules in
        the Grammars of Negro Speakers", in Project Literacy Report
        No. 8. Ithaca, Cornell University.

Labov, William, Paul Cohen and Clarence Robins
1965   A Preliminary Study of the Structure of English Used by Negro
        and Puerto Rican Speakers in New York City. Final Report,
        Cooperative Research Project No. 3091, Office of Education.

Labov, William, Paul Cohen, Clarence Robins and John Lewis
    1968   A Study of the Non-Standard English of Negro and Puerto
            Rican Speakers in New York City. Final Report, Cooperative
            Research Project No. 3288, Office of Education.

Lamb, Sydney M.
    1964   "On Alternation, Transformation, Realization and Stratifi-
            cation", in Monograph Series on Languages and Linguistics,
            Vol. 17, ed. by C.I.J.M. Stuart. Washington, D.C., George-
            town University Press.

    1966a   "Prolegomena to a Theory of Phonology", Language 42:536-573.

    1966b   Outline of Stratificational Grammar. Washington, D. C.,
            Georgetown University Press.

Landecker, Werner S.
    1960   "Class Boundaries", American Sociological Review 25:868-877.

LePage, R.B.
    1964   The National Language Question: Linguistic Problems of
            Newly Independent States. London, Oxford University
            Press.

Lenski, Gerhard
    1961   The Religious Factor. Rev. ed. New York, Doubleday.

Levine, Lewis and Harry J. Crockett, Jr.
    1966   "Speech Variation in a Piedmont Community: Postvocalic r",
            Sociological Inquiry 35:204-226.

    1967   "Friends Influence on Speech", Sociological Inquiry
            37:109-128.

Loban, Walter
    1966   Problems in Oral English. Champaign, National Council of
            Teachers of English.

Loflin, Marvin D.
    1967a   "A Teaching Problem in Nonstandard Negro English", English
            Journal 56:1312-1314.

    1967b   "On the Structure of the Verb in a Dialect of American
            Negro English". Office of Naval Research, Group Psychology
            Branch, Contract No. 2296 (02), Technical Report No. 26.

    forthcoming "Negro Nonstandard and Standard English: Same or
            Different Deep Structure", in Current Viewpoints on Non-
            Standard 'Be', ed. by Roger W. Shuy and Ralph W. Fasold.
            Washington, D.C., Center for Applied Linguistics.

Loman, Bengt
  1967a Conversations in a Negro American Dialect. Washington,
         D.C., Center for Applied Linguistics.

  1967b "Intonation Patterns in a Negro American Dialect: A Pre-
         liminary Report." Washington, D.C., Center for Applied
         Linguistics, Unpublished manuscript.

McDavid, Raven I., Jr.
  1948   "Postvocalic r in South Carolina: A Social Analysis",
         American Speech 23:194-203.

  1965   "American Social Dialects", College English 26:254-260.

  1967   "Historical, Regional, and Social Variation", Journal of
         English Linguistics 1:25-40.

McDavid, Raven I., Jr., ed.
  1963   The American Language, by Henry L. Mencken, Abridged.
         New York, Harcourt, Brace.

McDavid, Raven I., Jr. and Virginia Glenn McDavid
  1951   The Relationship of the Speech of American Negroes to the
         Speech of Whites", American Speech 26:3-17.

Myrdal, Gunnar
  1944   An American Dilemma. New York, Harper & Row.

Pederson, Lee A.
  1965   The Pronunciation of English in Metropolitan Chicago,
         Publication of the American Dialect Society No. 44.
         University, University of Alabama Press.

Pickford, Glenna Ruth
  1956   "American Linguistic Geography: A Sociological Appraisal",
         Word 12:211-235.

Putnam, George N. and Edna M. O'Hern
  1955   "The Status Significance of an Isolated Urban Dialect",
         Language 34, No. 4, Part 2.

Sharp, Harry
  1960   "Estimates of the Distribution of the White and Non-white
         Population of Greater Detroit: 1940-1960." Ann Arbor,
         Detroit Area Study, Mimeographed.

Shuy, Roger W.
  1969   "A Linguistic Background for Developing Beginning Reading
         Materials for Black Children", in Teaching Black Children
         to Read, ed. by Joan C. Baratz and Roger W. Shuy. Washing-
         ton, D.C., Center for Applied Linguistics.

Shuy, Roger W., Walter A. Wolfram and William K. Riley
  1967   Linguistic Correlates of Social Stratification in Detroit
          Speech. Final Report, Cooperative Research Project No.
          6-1347, United States Office of Education.

  1968   Field Techniques in an Urban Language Study. Washington,
          D.C., Center for Applied Linguistics.

Shuy, Roger W., Joan C. Baratz and Walter A. Wolfram
  1969   Sociolinguistic Factors in Speech Identification. Final
          Report, Research Project No. MH 15048-01, National Institute
          of Mental Health.

Stewart, William A.
  1962   "An Outline of Linguistic Typology for Describing Multi-
          lingualism", in Study of the Role of Second Languages,
          ed. by Frank A. Rice. Washington, D.C., Center for Applied
          Linguistics.

  1964a   Non-Standard Speech and the Teaching of English. Washington,
          D.C., Center for Applied Linguistics.

  1964b   "Urban Negro Speech: Sociolinguistic Factors Affecting
          English Teaching", in Social Dialects and Language Learning,
          ed. by Roger W. Shuy. Champaign, National Council of
          Teachers of English.

  1966a   "Nonstandard Speech Patterns", Baltimore Bulletin of Edu-
          cation 43:52-65.

  1966b   "Social Dialect", in Research Planning Conference on Language
          Development in Disadvantaged Children. New York, Yeshiva
          University.

  1967   "Sociolinguistic Factors in the History of American Negro
          Dialects", The Florida FL Reporter 5, No. 2:11, 22, 24, 26.

  1968   "Continuity and Change in American Negro Dialects", The
          Florida FL Reporter 6, No. 1:3-4, 14-16, 18.

  1969   "On the Use of Negro Dialect in the Teaching of Reading",
          in Teaching Black Children to Read, ed. by Joan C. Baratz
          and Roger W. Shuy. Washington, D.C., Center for Applied
          Linguistics.

Taber, Charles R.
  1966   The Structure of Sango Narrative. Hartford Studies in Lin-
          guistics No. 17. Hartford, The Hartford Seminary Foundation.

Templin, Mildred C.
  1957   Certain Language Skills in Children: Their Development and
          Interrelationships. Minneapolis, University of Minnesota
          Press.

Trager, George L. and Henry Lee Smith, Jr.
1951 An Outline of English Structure. Norman, Battenburg Press.

U.S. Commission on Civil Rights
1967 Racial Isolation in the Public Schools. Washington, D.C.,
      U.S. Government Printing Office.

U.S. Department of Commerce, Bureau of the Census
1960a Census Tracts: Detroit, Michigan. Washington, D.C., U.S.
      Government Printing Office.

1960b United States Census of Housing: 1960; Detroit, Michigan,
      Area. Washington, D.C., U.S. Government Printing Office.

1960c Mobility for States and State Economic Areas. Washington,
      D.C., U.S. Government Printing Office.

1960d United States Census of Population: 1960; State of Birth.
      Washington, D.C., U.S. Government Printing Office.

1960e United States Census of Population: 1960; Michigan.
      Washington, D.C., U.S. Government Printing Office.

Weinreich, Uriel
1953 Languages in Contact. The Hague, Mouton & Co.

Williamson, Juanita V.
1961 A Phonological and Morphological Study of the Speech of the
      Negro of Memphis, Tennessee. Ann Arbor, Unpublished doctoral
      dissertation, University of Michigan.

Wise, Claude Merton
1957 Applied Phonetics. Englewood Cliffs, Prentice-Hall.

Wolfram, Walter A. and Ralph W. Fasold
1969 "Toward Reading Materials for Speakers of Black English:
      Three Linguistically Appropriate Passages", in Teaching
      Black Children to Read, ed. by Joan C. Baratz and Roger W.
      Shuy. Washington, D.C., Center for Applied Linguistics.

Yuker, Harold E.
1958 A Guide to Statistical Calculations. New York, G.P. Putnam.

Zengel, Margorie
1961 "Literacy as a Factor in Language Change", American Anthro-
      pologist 64:132-139.